Building
Academic Fluency

Kathleen A. Romstedt

Gary W. Wolek

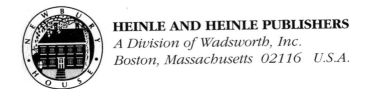

HEINLE AND HEINLE PUBLISHERS
A Division of Wadsworth, Inc.
Boston, Massachusetts 02116 U.S.A.

Publisher: Stanley J. Galek
Editorial Director: David C. Lee
Assistant Editor: Ken Mattsson
Editorial Production Manager: Elizabeth Holthaus
Production Editor: Kristin Thalheimer
Manufacturing Coordinator: Jerry Christopher
Production Coordination: Robert Ventre Associates, Inc.
Illustration: Jim Roldan
Interior Design: Amick Communications
Cover Design: Hannus Design Associates
Manufactured in the United States of America

Heinle & Heinle Publishers is a division of Wadsworth, Inc.

Library of Congress Cataloging-in-Publication Data
Romstedt, Kathleen.
    Building academic fluency/Kathleen A. Romstedt, Gary W. Wolek.
        p. cm.
    ISBN 0–8384–3412–6
    1. English language—Textbooks for foreign speakers.
    2. English language—Rhetoric.
    3. College readers.
II. Wolek, Gary W. II. Title.
PE1128.R636   1992
428.2'4—dc20
                                                    92–2875
                                                    CIP

10   9   8   7   6   5   4   3   2   1

Acknowledgments

We wish to express our gratitude to Maggie Barbieri for her willingness to consider a new approach to grammar instruction and for her help and understanding during the writing of this book. We also wish to thank our new editor, David Lee, and the staff of Heinle and Heinle Publishers, Inc. for taking over our project so efficiently. The following reviewers provided us with valuable comments during the development of our manuscript: Marjorie Fuchs, Virginia D. Lezhnev, Tamara Lovell, William Rindfleisch, and Barbara Robinson.

In addition, we wish to express our appreciation for the valuable suggestions and friendly encouragement we received from our colleagues in ESL Programs at The Ohio State University. We are especially grateful to Bill Holschuh and Robert Kantor.

Our special thanks go to our friends and families, whose support made this book possible.

Contents

Introduction

Building Academic Fluency offers a content-based approach to grammar instruction designed specifically for the college-bound adult learner at the high-beginning to intermediate levels of English study. It combines high-interest content with a focus on a selected set of grammatical patterns which occur naturally therein. This combination provides students with the opportunity to use language within a familiar, yet cognitively demanding framework that has an academic orientation.

THE APPROACH

This text is designed for students who are studying English prior to entering an undergraduate or graduate program of academic study at universities or colleges where courses are taught in English. With this in mind, we have employed a content-based approach that draws on the academic interests and backgrounds of these students. This approach emphasizes natural language usage that is relevant to students' goals. Students at the beginning and intermediate levels of instruction typically lack the language necessary to study grammar analytically. The philosophy reflected in this book emphasizes as primary the development of fluency and a broad language base as a foundation for productive accuracy of grammatical form.

The content-based approach employed here offers several advantages. First, it seeks to tap into students' cognitive backgrounds, thereby reducing anxiety often raised by the prospect of dealing with an unfamiliar topic in a new language. Second, it supplies abundant comprehensible input in many forms. In this text, content is presented in a variety of formats, taking into account differences in students' learning styles, thereby allowing for maximized individual progress. In addition, while focusing on academic content, students are actively reading, hearing, speaking, and writing. They work alone, in pairs, in small groups, and with the whole class. Suggestions for community contact activities are provided in the accompanying Instructor's Manual for every unit. These provide students with the opportunities to use English with native speakers, creating a flexible and communicative language learning environment which increases the opportunity for natural language production.

THE TEXT

The text consists of eight content units which are designed to provide the most natural environment for modeling and practicing specific grammatical patterns. The patterns are not presented with the usual lengthy and often confusing explanations seen in traditional grammar texts. Instead of concentrating on "the rules," the students are given the opportunity to see and hear the patterns in readings and lectures, to use them informally in class discussion, to discuss them as needed with the teacher, and to use them in context. Throughout the text, grammar patterns are recycled in new contexts to facilitate the students' acquisition of the structures.

The topics of the content units were selected not only to provide a background for the structures presented, but also to reflect the academic orientation of the students. The topics include plant life, food and nutrition, weather and climate, agriculture, small-town history, architecture, stress, and advertising. The teacher should not be concerned about lack of expertise in these areas. In nearly all cases, educated adults will have an existing background knowledge of these topics. It has been our experience that students are very willing to share their own expertise and opinions with the class, leading to many instances of cooperative learning in which even the most reticent student is able to participate.

Each chapter is organized into three sections which follow a sequence of presentation beginning with practical concepts and ending with an abstract process or idea. For example, the first chapter, Plant Life, begins with discussion and classification of types of plants, moves on to the identification of the parts of plants and their functions, and finally ends with the process of photosynthesis. In this way, each chapter presents a continuum along which the students' language becomes more fluent and grammatically sophisticated. Each chapter contains some or all of the following types of exercises:

Warm-up: This activity is essential for successful entry into the content. It sets the scene for the section and stimulates the students' background knowledge of the topic.

Readings: These are found throughout each chapter. They provide students with basic, even familiar information about the topic in English. They are intended to be a source of information for discussion, group work, and writing.

Lectures: At least one lecture is included in each chapter. They are limited in length and are intended to serve as an additional source of information for the students. In addition, the lectures allow students to hear the grammatical structures being used in a natural context.

Oral Practice: A variety of oral exercises, ranging from a simple question–answer format to individual presentations to be given to the class, provide students with the opportunity to practice the structures in each section in relationship to the content covered by the chapter.

Written Practice: Written exercises range from simple mechanical manipulation of structures to directed paragraph writing. The content of each chapter serves as the basis for creative use of the structures being practiced.

While using *Building Academic Fluency*, teachers are encouraged to approach the activities and patterns in this text creatively. Wherever possible, content should be expanded in response to student interest, for when students and teachers interact with content, real language learning occurs.

Kathleen A. Romstedt
Gary W. Wolek

FIGURE 1.1   Plant Life

Plant Life

CHAPTER 1

Types of Plants

LESSON 1

A. WARM-UP: *ON YOUR OWN*

Before class, take a walk near your house or your school. Look for different types of plants, large and small. On the chart below, write notes about each plant. Then, share your descriptions with your classmates and teacher in class.

CHART 1.1

Type of Plant	Size	Colors	Leaf Shape	Other Notes

B. FOCUS VOCABULARY: *ON YOUR OWN*

On the lines below, write down new words that you learn in class. Add to your list as you study types of plants. Focus on new nouns and adjectives.

_____ _____ _____

_____ _____ _____

_____ _____ _____

_____ _____ _____

C. DISCUSSION: *WITH YOUR CLASS*

Talk with your classmates about plants. Answer these questions.

1. How many different types of plants did you and your classmates find?
2. Can you divide the plants into different categories? What are the categories?
3. What is the simplest category you can make?

Plants

Types of Plants

Plants are found in almost every part of the world. Only a few places are too hot, too cold, or too dry for them to grow. Plants can grow anywhere there is enough sunlight, food, and water. In fact, they can grow in the desert or under the sea. There are plants of almost every shape, size, and color. Some plants are very old and very large, while other plants are very small.

There are more than 350,000 different types of plants on earth. Each type is called a species. Although there are many species of plants, there are only two main groups of plants: simple and advanced. Simple plants reproduce by cell division. They do not produce seeds. Algae and fungi are simple plants. Seaweed is a type of algae and mushrooms are a type of fungi.

Advanced plants produce seeds. Trees and flowering plants, which both produce seeds, are advanced plants. Some trees, especially fruit and nut trees, have flowers. Flowering plants include many vegetable plants, bushes, and flowers.

Trees

Trees are the biggest plants. They grow in almost every part of the world, but they cannot grow in extremely cold climates. Two main types of trees grow in North America: deciduous and coniferous.

Deciduous trees have broad flat leaves. Their leaves are usually green in the summer and change color in the fall. In the winter, the leaves fall off the trees. New leaves grow again in the spring. Coniferous trees have long thin leaves called needles. The needles stay green all year and do not fall off in the winter. The seeds of coniferous trees grow inside cones.

The Importance of Plants

Plants are very important to us. They provide food, shelter, clothing, and other products. They supply the oxygen that we need to breathe. Life on earth would not be possible without plants.

E. COMPREHENSION: *ON YOUR OWN OR IN PAIRS*

E.1. True or False

Read each statement about the reading and circle True or False. If the statement is false, correct it.

MODEL: **Algae and fungi are advanced plants.**   True   (False)

Algae and fungi are simple plants.

1. Plants can grow almost anywhere in the world   **True**   **False**

2. Some plants can grow without much water.   **True**   **False**

3. Simple plants produce very small seeds.   **True**   **False**

4. Trees cannot grow in extremely cold climates.   **True**   **False**

5. There are three main types of trees in North America.   **True**   **False**

6. Trees produce oxygen.   **True**   **False**

7. Deciduous trees have long needles.   **True**   **False**

8. Coniferous trees stay green all year.   **True**   **False**

9. Deciduous trees do not lose their leaves in the fall.   **True**   **False**

10. Coniferous trees do not produce seeds.   **True**   **False**

E.2.   Charts

Using the information in the reading, complete the charts below.

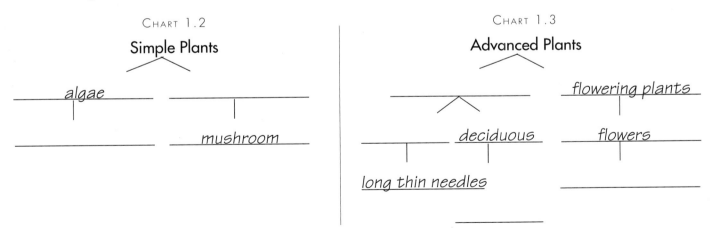

CHART 1.2

Simple Plants

algae

mushroom

CHART 1.3

Advanced Plants

flowering plants

deciduous   _flowers_

long thin needles

F.   DISCUSSION: *WITH YOUR CLASS*

With your classmates, answer these questions.

1. Are the plants where you live now the same or different from plants in your native country?
2. Is your country famous for any kind of plant or tree?
3. How do people in your country use plants?
4. What vegetables do people in your country like to grow in their vegetable gardens? What fruits?

Table 1.1   Study the patterns for using **there is** and **there are**.

Countable	**There**	**is** **isn't**	a cactus a rosebush	in my garden.
		are **aren't**	**some** strawberries **any** trees	
Noncountable	**There**	**is**	**some** corn	in my garden.
		isn't	**any** rice	
Interrogative	**Is**	**there**	a banana tree	in your garden?
	Are		**any** tomatoes	

G.   ORAL PRACTICE: *IN PAIRS*

1. At the top of the next page are pictures of two gardens. One shows a typical garden somewhere in North America, and the other shows a typical garden somewhere in Central America. Partner A looks at the picture of the North American garden and covers the picture of the Central American garden. Partner B looks at the picture of the Central American garden and covers the picture of the North American garden. First, Partner B asks Partner A questions about the North American garden. Partner A answers the questions, based on the picture. Then, Partner A asks Partner B questions about the Central American garden, which Partner B answers by looking at the picture. Use the information in Table 1.1 to help you form your questions and answers.

2. Now, repeat the process, but this time, Partner A looks at the picture of the Central American garden and asks Partner B questions about it; then, Partner B looks at the picture of the North American garden and asks Partner A questions about it. Again, refer to the information in Table 1.1 for help in forming your questions and answers.

MODEL: Partner B: Are there bananas in your garden?
Partner A: *No, there aren't*

H.   WRITTEN PRACTICE: *ON YOUR OWN*

Choose one of the gardens shown in Figure 1.2. Write eight sentences about whether or not these plants are in it. Follow the models.

MODELS: cactus: *There is a cactus in the garden.*

corn: *There is some corn in the garden.*

(Notice the use of some in an affirmative sentence.)

watermelons: *There aren't any watermelons.*

(Notice the use of any in a negative sentence.)

1. green beans: _____

2. coconut palm: _____

3. broccoli: _____

4. mango tree: _____

FIGURE 1.2 North American Garden   Central American Garden

5. lettuce: _____

6. tomatoes: _____

7. spinach: _____

8. orchids: _____

I. WRITTEN PRACTICE: *ON YOUR OWN*

Use the cues to write questions and answers with *there is* and *there are*.

__MODEL:__ leaves / trees <u>*Are there leaves on trees? Yes, there are.*</u>

1. flowers / apple trees _____

2. plant life / desert _____

3. trees / lake water _____

4. palm trees / desert _____

5. plants / ocean _____

6. flowers / all trees _____

7. needles / coniferous trees _____

8. seeds / coniferous cones _____

TABLE 1.2   **Study the patterns for using is and are.**

A mushroom	**is**	a fungus.
	isn't	an advanced plant.
Flowers	**are**	advanced plants.
	aren't	simple plants.

Asking questions with be.

Where	**is**	the stem?
	are	the roots?
Is Yes,	a mushroom a fungus? it **is**.	
Is No,	seaweed an advanced plant? it **isn't**.	
Are No,	fruit trees simple plants? they **aren't**.	
Are Yes,	fruit trees flowering plants? they **are**.	

J.   ORAL PRACTICE: *WITH YOUR CLASS*

Answer each question with a short answer. Add information to negative answers to make correct statements. Follow the model and the patterns in Table 1.2.

MODEL: Is moss an advanced plant?
       No, it isn't. Moss is a simple plant.

1. Are mushrooms simple plants?
2. Is an apple tree a simple plant?
3. Are roses advanced plants?
4. Are pine trees simple plants?
5. Is a fern a simple plant?
6. Is seaweed a simple plant?
7. Is seaweed an algae?
8. Is a carrot an advanced plant?
9. Are pine trees deciduous plants?
10. Are oak trees deciduous plants?
11. Are needles broad leaves?
12. Is a cherry tree a coniferous plant?

K.   ORAL PRACTICE: *IN PAIRS*

Use the cue words below to make questions. Take turns asking and answering questions. Follow the model and the patterns in Table 1.2.

MODEL: tree / simple plant
       Partner A: *Is a tree a simple plant?*
       Partner B: *No, it isn't.*

1. seaweed / a type of fungi
2. some plants / very old and large
3. algae / an advanced plant
4. many places / too cold for plants to grow
5. an apple tree / flowering plant
6. coniferous trees / green in winter
7. a deciduous leaf / broad and flat
8. deciduous trees / green all year
9. desert / too hot for plants to grow
10. flowering trees / coniferous

L. LISTENING PRACTICE: *WITH YOUR CLASS AND ON YOUR OWN*

L.1. Labeling Parts of Plants: *With Your Class*

What are the parts of plants? Look at the diagrams below. Fill in any parts that you know, using the words listed. Discuss this information with your classmates. Leave blank what you don't know.

branches	bark	flowers	leaves	stem	roots	trunk

FIGURE 1.3   Parts of plants

L.2. Listening: *On Your Own*

Listen to the lecture. Use the information in the lecture to finish filling in the parts of the tree and flowering plant in Exercise L.1. Make any necessary corrections.

M. ORAL PRACTICE: *WITH YOUR CLASS*

Ask and answer questions to check the information you heard in Exercise L. Use the correct form of the verb *be*.

MODEL: where / roots
              Student A: *Where are the roots?*
              Student B: *The roots are in the ground.*
                                OR
                        They are in the ground.

1. where / leaves of a flower
2. where / minerals
3. where / water
4. where / seeds
5. where / fruit
6. where / flowers
7. where / leaves of a tree
8. where / branches
9. where / bark

TABLE 1.3   **Study the patterns for using do and does.**

Does Yes,	a tree it **does**.	have roots?
Does No,	a tree it **doesn't**.	have a stem?
Do Yes,	plants they **do**.	need water?
Do No,	trees they **don't**.	have stems?

N.   ORAL PRACTICE: *IN PAIRS*

Ask and answer questions about the parts of trees and flowers. Use the information in the diagram on page 15 or your own knowledge. Use the correct form of the verb. Follow the models and the patterns in Table 1.3.

MODELS: tree / roots
  Partner A: *Does a tree have roots?*
  Partner B: *Yes, it does.*

  stem / bark
  Partner A: *Does a stem have bark?*
  Partner B: *No, it doesn't.*

1. plant / roots
2. plants / leaves
3. apple / seeds
4. trees / long roots
5. deciduous trees / needles

6. flowers / reproductive parts
7. tree / bark
8. coniferous trees / cones
9. flower / trunk
10. trees / stems

O.   WRITTEN PRACTICE: *ON YOUR OWN*

Using all the information you have learned in this chapter, write a sentence to answer each of these questions.

1. What do the roots of a plant do?

_____

2. What do we call the stem of a tree?

_____

3. What do the roots absorb from the soil?

_____

4. Which part of the plant uses the energy from sunlight to make food?

_____

5. Which part of a tree protects its trunk?

_____

6. Which parts of a deciduous tree fall off in the winter?

_____

7. What do we call the leaves of a pine tree?

_____

8. Which part of the tree is the most important part?

_____

TABLE 1.4   Study the patterns for talking about **facts**, **habits**, or **everyday actions**.

A coniferous tree	**stays**	green all year.
The roots of a plant	**absorb**	water.

<u>SPELLING RULE:</u>   Consonant +**y** becomes -**ies**.   **carries**
Vowel +**y** only adds -**s**.   **stays**

P.   WRITTEN PRACTICE: *ON YOUR OWN*

Use the information in Table 1.4 to complete these sentences. Use the correct form of the verbs in parentheses.

1. The roots _____ (hold) the plants in the ground.

2. The roots _____ (absorb) water and minerals from the soil.

3. The stem _____ (carry) water and minerals to the leaves.

4. A leaf _____ (use) energy from the sun to make food.

5. The leaves _____ (take in) carbon dioxide and _____ (give off) oxygen.

6. Flowers _____ (be) the reproductive part of the tree.

7. A tree _____ (have) a trunk.

8. Branches _____ (grow) outside the trunk.

9. Bark _____ (protect) the trunk.

10. Every tree _____ (have) a differently shaped leaf.

Q. WRITTEN PRACTICE: *ON YOUR OWN*

Use the words below and the information from Table 1.4 to make statements. If the information is the same for trees and flowers, use *both*. If it is different, use *but*. Follow the model.

MODEL: trees / leaves / flowers / leaves

_____ *Both trees and flowers have leaves.* _____

trees / trunks / flowers / stems

_____ *Trees have trunks but flowers have stems.* _____

1. trees / roots / flowers / roots

_____

2. trees / bark / flowers / stem

_____

3. trees / seeds / flowers / seeds

_____

4. flowers / stems / trees / branches

_____

5. trees / leaves / flowers / leaves

_____

6. flowers / small short roots / trees / large strong roots

_____

7. trees / large trunks / flowers / small stems

_____

8. trees / fruit / plants / fruit

_____

The Uses of Plants
LESSON 2

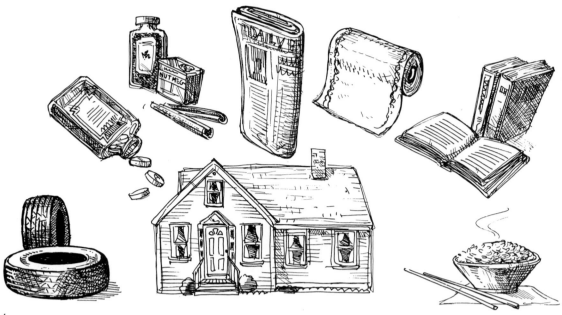

FIGURE 1.4

A. WARM-UP: *WITH YOUR CLASS*

Look at the pictures above. Talk with your classmates about how plants are used. Try to answer these questions.

1. How do people use plants?
2. Find two things in your classroom that come from plants. What are they? What kinds of plants do they come from?
3. Is there anything on or in a car that comes from plants?
4. Do people use plants when they are sick? If so, what kinds of plants do they use?

B. FOCUS VOCABULARY: *ON YOUR OWN*

On the lines below, write down new words that you learn in class. Add to your list as you study the uses of plants. Focus on new verbs and adjectives.

_____   _____   _____

_____   _____   _____

_____   _____   _____

_____   _____   _____

_____   _____   _____

_____   _____   _____

_____   _____   _____

C. LISTENING PRACTICE: *ON YOUR OWN*

Listen to what your teacher tells you about the uses of plants and their parts. Write down the main ideas on the lines below.

fruits _____

seeds _____

trunk _____

bark _____

sap _____

leaves / flowers _____

green plants _____

D. WRITTEN PRACTICE: *ON YOUR OWN*

Answer these questions about the uses of plants. Use the information from your notes, above.

1. What part of the tree gives us wood for building houses?

_____

2. When do people use herbs and spices?

_____

3. What part of the plant does rice come from?

_____

4. Where does aspirin come from?

_____

5. What part of the plant does tea come from?

_____

6. What do people make with wood?

_____

7. How do people use sap?

_____

8. What do green plants supply?

_____

9. What kinds of plants do people eat?

_____

10. Where does paper come from?

_____

E. WRITTEN PRACTICE: *ON YOUR OWN*

Write sentences about the uses of plants. Use the words below.

MODEL: cacao tree / supply / chocolate

   The cacao tree supplies chocolate. _____

1. softwood / come from / coniferous trees

_____

2. people / cook / with herbs

_____

3. maple sugar trees / provide / sugar

_____

4. cinchona bark / supply / quinine

_____

5. spices / be / important / for cooking

_____

6. green plants / give off / oxygen

_____

7. a cotton plant / provide / fibers for cloth

_____

8. paper / be / a wood product

_____

9. plant / supply / many important medicines

_____

10. rubber / come from / sap

_____

TABLE 1.5   Study the patterns for using sentences with **because**.

An apple tree is important	**because**	it supplies	fruit.
Orange trees are important		they supply	

F.   ORAL PRACTICE: *WITH YOUR CLASS*

Tell why you think each of the following is important. Use because in your answer. Follow the model and the patterns in Table 1.5.

MODEL: orange trees
            Orange trees are important because they supply fruit.

1. coniferous trees
2. fruit trees
3. herbs
4. seeds
5. coffee trees
6. cotton plants
7. cacao trees
8. rubber trees
9. tea bushes
10. rosebushes

G.   WRITTEN PRACTICE: *ON YOUR OWN*

What plants grow in your native country? What are they used for? Fill in the chart below with notes about plants in your native country and their uses.

CHART 1.4

COUNTRY: _____	
Plant	Use

H.   ORAL PRACTICE: *IN PAIRS*

Use the information from Chart 1.4 to talk about plants and their uses. Follow the model. Take turns telling about the plants.

MODEL: Partner A: *Banana trees grow in Costa Rica.*
            Partner B: *What are they used for?*
            Partner A: *They provide fruit.*

Photosynthesis
LESSON 3

A.   WARM-UP: *WITH YOUR CLASS*

   1. What three things does a plant need to live?
   2. What part of the plant takes in water?
   3. Where do you think the plant makes its food?
   4. Are plants important to the atmosphere?

B.   READING

Photosynthesis

Photosynthesis is the process by which plants and trees make glucose, a simple sugar. This process is the main function of the leaves of plants. In order for photosynthesis to occur, there must be sunlight. The leaves of a plant contain a green pigment called chlorophyll. Green plants absorb energy from sunlight and combine it with water (H_2O) and carbon dioxide (CO_2) to make glucose ($C_6H_{12}O_6$). When the plants make glucose, they release oxygen (O) into the atmosphere. Human beings and animals breathe in oxygen and release carbon dioxide. Plants use CO_2 in photosynthesis. This is a continuous cycle. It supports life on earth for all living things.

photosynthesis process

sunlight

chlorophyll

glucose

water

respiration

animals
release carbon dioxide

plants
release oxygen

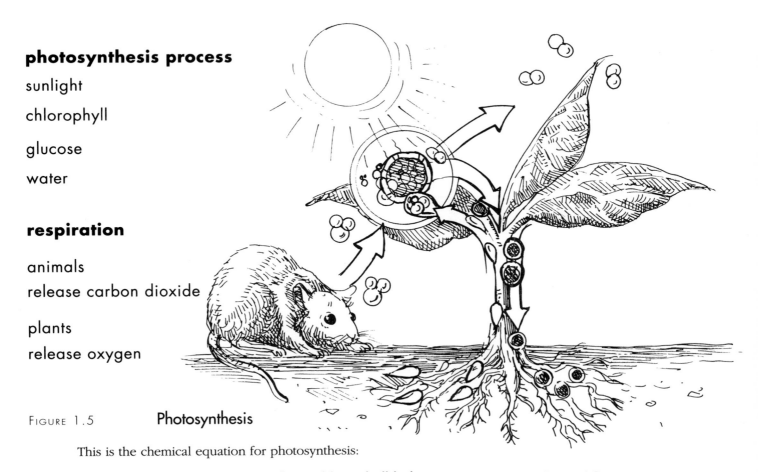

FIGURE 1.5   Photosynthesis

This is the chemical equation for photosynthesis:

$$6CO_2 + 6H_2O + e- \text{ from chlorophyll light energy} \rightarrow C_6H_{12}O_6 + 6O_2$$

C. FOCUS VOCABULARY: *ON YOUR OWN*

On the lines below, write down new words that you learn in class. Add to your list as you study photosynthesis. Focus on nouns and verbs.

_____   _____   _____

_____   _____   _____

_____   _____   _____

_____   _____   _____

_____   _____   _____

_____   _____   _____

D. COMPREHENSION: *ON YOUR OWN*

D.1. True or False

Look at each of the following statements. Remember what you have learned about plants. If the statement is true, write a short sentence to show that you agree. If it is false, write a short sentence to show that you disagree. Then write another sentence, making the statement true. Use complete sentences.

MODELS: Human beings need oxygen. _____*Yes, they do.*_____

Leaves release carbon dioxide. _____*No, they don't. They release oxygen.*_____

A plant uses carbon dioxide. _____*Yes, it does.*_____

A tree needs oxygen._____*No, it doesn't. It needs carbon dioxide.*_____

1. Roots absorb water.

_____

2. Photosynthesis requires sunlight.

_____

3. Roots bring glucose to the leaves.

_____

4. Chlorophyll is green.

_____

5. Water molecules contain hydrogen and carbon.

_____

6. Leaves send water to the roots.

_____

7. Leaves take in oxygen from the air.

_____

8. Carbon dioxide is necessary for photosynthesis.

_____

9. Photosynthesis is a process.

_____

10. Photosynthesis is important for human life.

_____

D.2. Comprehension Questions

Write a complete sentence to answer each of the following questions about the process of photosynthesis.

1. What things are necessary for photosynthesis to occur?

_____

2. What makes leaves green?

_____

3. What does chlorophyll do?

_____

4. How many hydrogen molecules are there in water? (Try to guess.)

_____

5. What kind of food does a leaf make?

_____

6. Does a tree use oxygen?

_____

E.   ORAL PRACTICE: *IN PAIRS*

Look at Columns A and B below. Partner A covers Column B and uses the information in the sentence in Column A to ask questions. Partner B answers the questions with the information in Column B. Follow the model.

MODEL:

Column A

Sap is _____. (what)

Column B

a liquid

Partner A: *What is sap?*
Partner B: *Sap is a liquid.*

Column A

1. Chlorophyll is _____. (what)
2. Leaves are green _____. (when)
3. The roots are _____. (where)
4. Chlorophyll is _____. (where)
5. The sap is _____. (where)

Column B

a green, chemical substance
in the summer
in the ground
in the leaves
in the trunk and branches

Now, change roles with your partner.

6. Chlorophyll is _____. (what color)
7. The leaves are _____. (where)
8. $C_6H_{12}O_6$ is _____. (what)
9. Sugar is _____. (what)
10. Photosynthesis is _____. (what)

green
on the branches
glucose / sugar
food
a process

F.   RETELLING THE SEQUENCE: *IN PAIRS*

Work with your partner to fill in the steps of photosynthesis on the diagram below. Use the words listed and write as much as you can. Check your work by looking at the diagram on page 23.

animals
breathe in oxygen
chlorophyll
glucose
photosynthesis process
plants
release carbon dioxide
release oxygen
respiration
sunlight
water

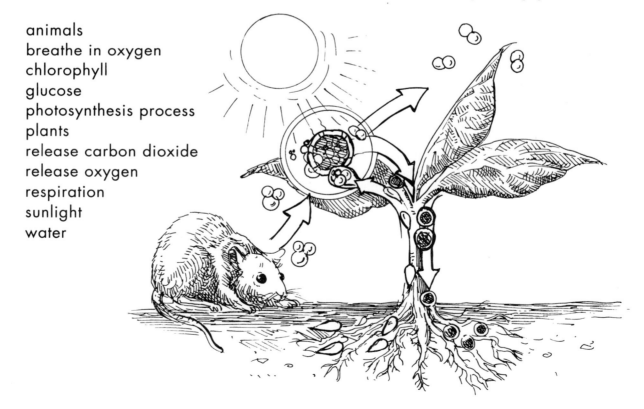

G. WRITTEN PRACTICE: *ON YOUR OWN*

Now practice writing a paragraph about the the process of photosynthesis. Use the information in the diagram above. Try to include some of these sequence expressions. (The first sentence has been done for you.)

     Second   Then   Next   After that   Finally

First, the plant takes in water and sunlight. _____

_____

_____

_____

_____

_____

_____

_____

Figure 2.1   Food and Nutrition

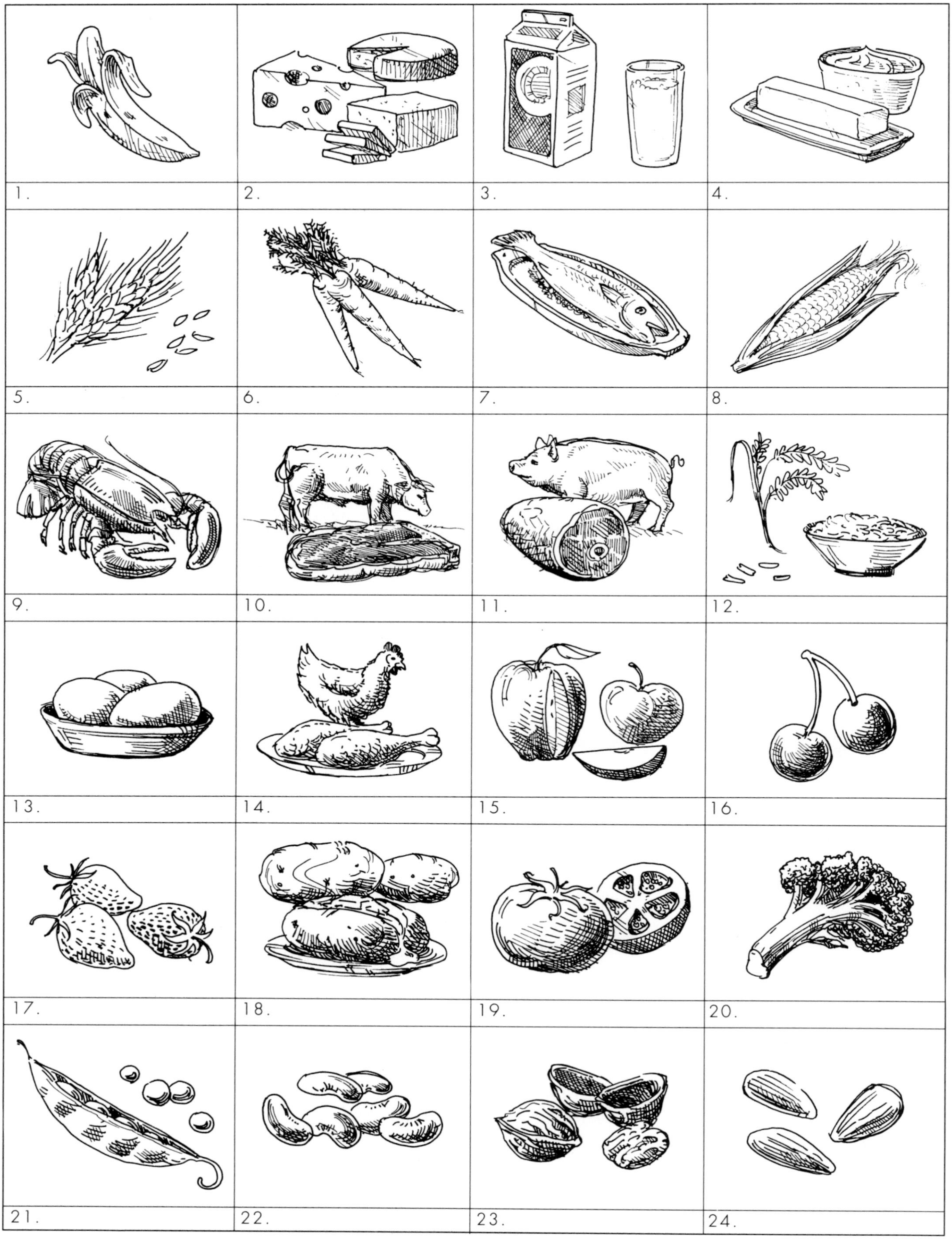

1.	2.	3.	4.
5.	6.	7.	8.
9.	10.	11.	12.
13.	14.	15.	16.
17.	18.	19.	20.
21.	22.	23.	24.

Food and Nutrition
CHAPTER 2

Types of Food
LESSON 1

A.   WARM-UP: *IN SMALL GROUPS*

Can you identify the foods in the pictures on page 28? With your group, label the food that you can identify. Check your answers with your teacher.

TABLE 2.1   **Study the patterns for countable and noncountable nouns.**

Singular	a banana one banana	rice a cup of rice some rice
Plural	bananas two bananas some bananas	

B.   ORAL PRACTICE: *WITH YOUR CLASS*

Check your food labels in Exercise A by asking and answering questions about the food pictures. Tell what type of food is in each picture. Choose from these categories.

meat	vegetable	dairy product
fruit	poultry	nut
seafood	legume	grain

Follow the models. If you don't know what a food is, try to guess. Follow the models and the patterns in Table 2.1.

MODELS:

Student A:	*What is in picture 1?*
Student B:	*There is a banana.*
Student A:	*What is a banana?*
Student B:	*It's a fruit.*
Student A:	*What is in picture 6?*
Student B:	*There are carrots.*
Student A:	*What are carrots?*
Student B:	*They are vegetables.*
Student A:	*What is in picture 12?*
Student B:	*There is rice.*
Student A:	*What is in picture 12?*
Student B:	*It's grain.*

C. FOCUS VOCABULARY: *ON YOUR OWN*

On the lines below, write the new words that you learn in class. Add to your list as you study about types of food. Focus on countable and noncountable nouns.

_____   _____   _____

_____   _____   _____

_____   _____   _____

_____   _____   _____

_____   _____   _____

D. WRITTEN PRACTICE: *ON YOUR OWN*

On the chart below, write the names of the food in the pictures on page 28. Choose the appropriate category. You will write in some categories more than once.

CHART 2.1

Meat	
Poultry	
Seafood	
Dairy Product	
Grain	
Fruit	
Vegetable	
Legume	
Nut	

TABLE 2.2 **Study the patterns for asking questions about kinds of food.**

Singular	What category	is	rice	in?
Plural		are	carrots	
Singular	What type of food	is	rice	?
Plural		are	carrots	

D.1. Answering Questions

Use the information from Chart 2.1 to answer the following questions. Follow the models and the patterns in Table 2.2.

MODELS: Q: What category are carrots in?

A: _____ *Carrots are in the vegetable category.* _____

Q: What type of food are carrots?

A: _____ *Carrots are vegetables.* _____

Q: What category is rice in?

A: _____ *Rice is in the grain category.* _____

Q: What type of food is rice?

A: _____ *Rice is grain.* _____

1. Q: What category are potatoes in?

A: _____

2. Q: What category is milk in?

A: _____

3. Q: What type of food is beef?

A: _____

4. Q: What type of food are cherries?

A: _____

5. Q: What type of food are peas?

A: _____

6. Q: What category is chicken in?

A: _____

7. Q: What category are cashews in?

A: _____

8. Q: What type of food are tomatoes?

A: _____

9. Q: What type of food is cabbage?

A: _____

10. Q: What category are clams in?

A: _____

D.2. Asking and Answering Questions

Use the following words to write questions. Write answers with your information from Chart 2.1.

MODELS: What category / oranges / in

        Q: _____ *What category are oranges in?* _____

        A: _____ *Oranges are in the fruit category.* _____

        What type of food / corn

        Q: _____ *What type of food is corn?* _____

        A: _____ *Corn is grain.* _____

1. What category / apples / in

    Q: _____

    A: _____

2. What type of food / onions

    Q: _____

    A: _____

3. What category / turkey / in

    Q: _____

    A: _____

4. What category / beans / in

    Q: _____

    A: _____

5. What type of food / butter

    Q: _____

    A: _____

6. What type of food / ham

    Q: _____

    A: _____

E. READING   *Food*

Food is necessary for all living things. It supplies the energy that living things need for growth. Green plants can produce their food for themselves with the process of photosynthesis. People and animals, however, cannot make their own food. They must eat plants or other animals.

Some animals eat only one kind of food. Cows, for example, eat mainly grass. Animals which eat mainly plants in their diet are called herbivores. Other animals, such as lions, eat mainly meat. They are hunters that kill and eat other animals. Animals that eat mainly meat are called carnivores. People are different from other animals because they regularly eat both plants and meat. People are called omnivores because they eat all types of food: meat, poultry, seafood, dairy products, grain, fruit, vegetables, legumes, and nuts.

Food is not the same in every country because the same types of food do not grow in every climate. For example, bananas grow in a tropical climate, apples grow in a cool climate, and figs grow in a dry climate. People traditionally eat the food that grows in their climate. For this reason, people in different parts of the world have different kinds of food in their diets.

F. COMPREHENSION: *On Your Own*

F.1. True or False

Read each statement about the reading and then circle *True* or *False*. If the statement is false, correct it.

1. Cows eat all types of food.   **True**   **False**

_____

2. Food supplies energy for growth.   **True**   **False**

_____

3. Animals cannot produce food by photosynthesis.   **True**   **False**

_____

4. People all over the world eat the same kinds of food.   **True**   **False**

_____

5. Herbivores eat only meat.   **True**   **False**

_____

6. The same types of food do not grow in every climate.   **True**   **False**

_____

7. Lions are carnivores.   **True**   **False**

_____

8. Green plants do not need food.   **True**   **False**

9. Omnivores eat both plants and animals.   **True**   **False**

10. Figs are a traditional food in a dry climate.   **True**   **False**

F.2. Comprehension Questions

Answer the following questions using the information from the reading. Write a sentence to answer each question.

1. Why do living things need food?

   _____

2. Why is it possible for green plants to make their own food?

   _____

3. How are herbivores different from carnivores?

   _____

4. Why is the human diet different from the diet of most animals?

   _____

5. Why don't people eat the same food in all parts of the world?

   _____

G.   DISCUSSION: *WITH YOUR CLASS*

Take turns asking and answering these questions.

1. What other animals besides cows are mainly herbivores?
2. What other animals besides lions are mainly carnivores?
3. Is food in the United States different from food in your country? How is it different?
4. What is your favorite food? Is it easy to find in the United States?
5. What is a typical meal in your country?

1.   2.   3.   4.   5.   6.   7.   8.   9.   10.   11.   12.   13.   14.   15.   16.

FIGURE 2.2

H.   ORAL PRACTICE: *WITH YOUR CLASS*

H.1. Identification

Look at the pictures above. Can you identify the foods?

H.2. Countable and Noncountable Nouns

Review the countable and noncountable patterns in Table 2.1, on page 29. Practice asking questions with the phrase *What kind of food is...?* Then, take turns asking and answering the questions. Follow the models. Choose foods from the list below. (Add the new food items to Chart 2.1, on page 30.)

MODELS: a banana
      Student A: *What kind of food is a banana?*
      Student B: *A banana is a fruit.*

    carrots
      Student A: *What kind of food are carrots?*
      Student B: *Carrots are vegetables.*

    chicken
      Student A: *What kind of food is chicken?*
      Student B: *Chicken is poultry.*

1. a pineapple	5. tuna	9. lettuce	13. cucumbers
2. lamb	6. cheese	10. grapes	14. a watermelon
3. a pear	7. a grapefruit	11. shrimp	15. lentils
4. wheat	8. cherries	12. an eggplant	16. cauliflower

FIGURE 2.3

I. ORAL PRACTICE: *WITH YOUR CLASS*

I.1. Identification

Look at the pictures of places that food grows. With your teacher, fill in the missing words.

1. _____ and _____ grow on trees.

2. _____ grows in water.

3. _____ and _____ grow under the ground.

4. _____ and _____ grow on a stalk.

5. _____ and _____ grow on a vine.

6. _____ and _____ grow on a plant.

7. _____ grows in the ground.

TABLE 2.3   Study the patterns for **asking questions** about where food grows.

Singular	Where	does	wheat	grow?
Plural		do	peanuts	

I.2. Asking and Answering Questions

Look at the pictures in Exercise A and Exercise H on pages 28 and 35. Ask someone in your class a question about a plant product, using the phrase *Where does . . . grow?* or *Where do . . . grow?* If your classmate doesn't know the answer, ask the person to guess. Do you agree with the answer? Follow the models and the patterns in Table 2.3.

MODELS: wheat
            Student A: *Where does wheat grow?*
            Student B: *It grows on a stalk.*
                        OR
                    Wheat grows on a stalk.

            peanuts
            Student A: *Where do peanuts grow?*
            Student B: *They grow under the ground.*
                        OR
                    Peanuts grow under the ground.

TABLE 2.4   Study the patterns for **asking questions** about where animal products come from.

Singular	Where	does	milk	come from?
Plural		do	clams	

I.3. Asking and Answering Questions

Look at the pictures in Exercise A and Exercise H on pages 28 and 35. Which foods are animal products? Ask someone in your class a question about an animal product, using the phrase *Where does...come from?* or *Where do...come from?* If your classmate doesn't know, ask the person to guess. Do you agree with the answer? Follow the models and the patterns in Table 2.4.

MODELS: milk
            Student A: *Where does milk come from?*
            Student B: *It comes from a cow.*
                     OR
               Milk comes from a cow.

        clams
            Student A: *Where do clams come from?*
            Student B: *They come from the ocean.*
                     OR
               Clams come from the ocean.

J.   WRITTEN PRACTICE: *ON YOUR OWN*

J.1. Writing Questions and Answers

Write questions about where different kinds of plant products grow. Then write answers to the questions. If you don't know, try to guess. When you are finished, check your answers with your classmates' answers.

MODELS: oranges   Q: _____ *Where do oranges grow?* _____

               A: _____ *They grow on a tree.* _____

      OR
                   Oranges grow on a tree. _____

        corn: Q: _____ *Where does corn grow?* _____

               A: _____ *It grows on a stalk.* _____

      OR
                   Corn grows on a stalk. _____

1. apples   Q: _____

         A: _____

2. carrots   Q: _____

         A: _____

3. potatoes   Q: _____

         A: _____

4. wheat   Q: _____

         A: _____

5. rice   Q: _____

              A: _____

6. grapes   Q: _____

              A: _____

7. cabbage   Q: _____

              A: _____

8. lettuce   Q: _____

              A: _____

9. soybeans   Q: _____

              A: _____

10. coconuts Q: _____

              A: _____

J.2. Writing Questions and Answers

Write questions about where different kinds of animal products come from. Then write answers to the questions. If you don't know, try to guess. When you are finished, check your answers with your classmates' answers.

MODELS: milk   Q: *Where does milk come from?* _____

                  A: *It comes from a cow.* _____

          OR
                      Milk comes from a cow. _____

          shrimp Q: *Where do shrimp come from?* _____

                  A: *They come from the ocean.* _____

          OR
                      Shrimp come from the ocean. _____

1. beef   Q: _____

              A: _____

2. butter   Q: _____

              A: _____

3. lobsters   Q: _____

              A: _____

4. eggs   Q: _____

              A: _____

5. ham   Q: _____

              A: _____

K. ORAL AND WRITTEN PRACTICE

K.1. Oral Practice: *In Pairs*

Look at the model questions and answers below with your partner. Ask your partner questions from the list below, using the model. Do you agree with your partner's answer? Take turns asking and answering questions.

MODELS: bananas / under the ground
> Partner A: *Do bananas grow under the ground?*
> Partner B: *No, they don't. Bananas grow in trees.*

grapes / on vines
> Partner B: *Do grapes grow on vines?*
> Partner A: *Yes, they do. Grapes grow on vines.*

1. tomatoes / on plants
2. potatoes / on trees
3. beans / under the ground
4. apples / on a vine
5. strawberries / on plants
6. lettuce / in the ground
7. broccoli / in water
8. rice / under the ground
9. corn / on stalks
10. cabbage / on stalks

K.2. Written Practice: *On Your Own*

After you practice orally all the questions and answers in Exercise K.1., write each question and answer on the lines below.

1. Q: _____
   A: _____

2. Q: _____
   A: _____

3. Q: _____
   A: _____

4. Q: _____
   A: _____

5. Q: _____
   A: _____

6. Q: _____
   A: _____

7. Q: _____
   A: _____

8. Q: _____
   A: _____

9. Q: _____
   A: _____

10. Q: _____
    A: _____

TABLE 2.5   Study the patterns for **asking questions** about the color, shape, and size of food items.

Singular	What	color shape size	is	a cucumber?
Plural			are	oranges?

L.   ORAL PRACTICE: *IN PAIRS*

With your partner, practice asking questions about the color, the shape, and the size of different food items. Follow the models and the patterns in Table 2.5.

MODELS: what color / bananas
        Partner A: *What color are bananas?*
        Partner B: *Bananas are yellow.*
              OR
        They are yellow.

    what shape / a grapefruit
        Partner A: *What shape is a grapefruit?*
        Partner B: *A grapefruit is round.*
              OR
        It is round.

1. what color / strawberries
2. what color / an eggplant
3. what color / a potato
4. what color / corn
5. what color / carrots

6. what shape / an orange
7. what shape / an egg
8. what shape / cabbage
9. what size / a watermelon
10. what size / peas

M.   ORAL PRACTICE: *IN PAIRS*

Ask your partner a question about the underlined word or words in each sentence below. Decide which of the following question words or phrases you will use for your question.

What color?   What shape?   What size?   When?
What kind of food?   Where?   What?

Take turns asking the questions. Partner A keeps the book open while asking the question. Partner B listens to the question and answers it. Partner A asks questions for items 1–7. Then Partner B asks questions for items 8–14.

MODEL: Potatoes are <u>brown</u>.
        Partner A: *What color are potatoes?*
        Partner B: *Potatoes are brown.*
              OR
        They are brown.

1. Apples are <u>red</u>.
2. Oranges are <u>round</u>.
3. A watermelon is <u>large</u>.
4. Rice is <u>white</u>.
5. Pears grow <u>on trees</u>.
6. Ice cream is <u>a dairy product</u>.
7. Farmers sell pumpkins <u>in the autumn</u>.

8. Tomatoes are <u>red</u>.
9. Corn is <u>yellow</u>.
10. A watermelon is <u>big</u>.
11. Grapefruits are <u>round</u>.
12. Grapes grow <u>on vines</u>.
13. Turkey is <u>poultry</u>.
14. Farmers sell strawberries <u>in the summer</u>.

Nutrients in Food
LESSON 2

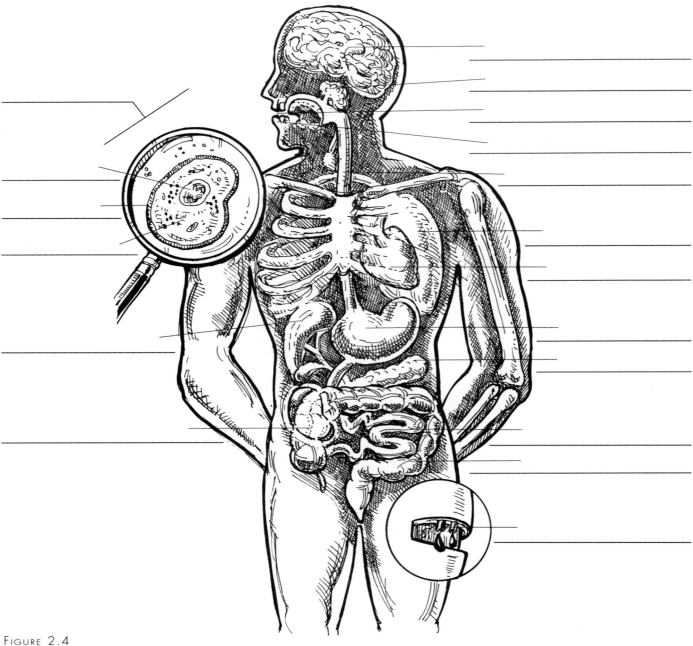

FIGURE 2.4

brain	blood cell	nucleus	heart	esophagus	large intestine
mouth	pancreas	enzymes	teeth	salivary glands	artery with blood cells
liver	stomach	kidneys	lungs	small intestine	cell membrane

A.   WARM-UP: *IN SMALL GROUPS*

Look at the picture above with your teacher. How many words do you know? Fill in the blanks with
the words that you already know. Compare your answers with your classmates' answers. Go over
the words with your class and your teacher.

B. FOCUS VOCABULARY: *ON YOUR OWN*

On the lines below, write down the new words that you learn in class. Add to your list as you study about food and nutrition. Focus on verbs and countable and noncountable nouns.

_____   _____   _____

_____   _____   _____

_____   _____   _____

_____   _____   _____

_____   _____   _____

_____   _____   _____

C. DISCUSSION: *WITH YOUR CLASS*

With your classmates, take turns asking and answering these questions.

1. What kind of food is good for building muscles?
2. Sometimes people say that they have tired blood. Do you know what they mean? What do they need to have healthy blood?
3. What mineral is important for strong bones and teeth?
4. What vitamin is good for a person who has a cold?
5. Do you know what these symbols mean: *Fe, Ca, S, P, Na?*
6. Can you name some internal organs? What are their functions?

D. LISTENING PRACTICE: *ON YOUR OWN AND IN SMALL GROUPS*

Your teacher will tell you about the nutrients that are in food. Add any new words to the vocabulary list you made in Exercise B. Your teacher will explain them while you are learning about nutrition. Write down the important ideas that you hear about nutrition in the chart below. Then, working in a small group, share your information with your classmates. Correct information in your chart and add information from your classmates' charts.

CHART 2.2

Nutrient		Importance	Sources
Protein			
Carbohydrates			
Fat			
Vitamins	A		
	C		
Minerals	Iron		
	Calcium		

E.   COMPREHENSION: *ON YOUR OWN*

E.1 True or False

Read each statement below and think about the lecture you heard about nutrition. Using the information in Chart 2.2 and your own knowledge, circle *True* or *False* after each statement below. If the statement is false, correct it.

1. Fat is important for strong bones.	**True**	**False**
2. Protein builds new cells in the body.	**True**	**False**
3. There are five main kinds of nutrients.	**True**	**False**
4. Fruit is a source of protein.	**True**	**False**
5. Fat protects the internal organs in the body.	**True**	**False**
6. Iron is a vitamin in citrus fruit.	**True**	**False**
7. Carbohydrates provide the body with energy.	**True**	**False**
8. Meat is rich in protein.	**True**	**False**
9. Vitamin A is important for blood cells.	**True**	**False**
10. People need a variety of food every day.	**True**	**False**

E.2. Comprehension Questions

Answer the following questions about nutrition with information from Chart 2.2 and your own knowledge.

1. What kinds of food supply carbohydrates?

2. Why is fat an important nutrient?

3. Which nutrient helps to build strong bones and teeth?

4. What kinds of food are good sources of iron?

5. Which nutrients do yellow and green vegetables provide?

_____

6. Why are carbohydrates important?

_____

7. What kinds of food are rich in vitamin C?

_____

8. What does vitamin A do for the body?

_____

9. What gives the body energy?

_____

10. Why is it necessary to eat many different kinds of food daily?

_____

F. DISCUSSION: *WITH YOUR CLASS*

1. What other vitamins can you name? Why are they important?
2. What other minerals can you name? Why are they important?
3. What are the typical sources of the five main nutrients in your diet in your country?
4. Doctors say that the typical American diet contains too much fat. What are some American foods that contain a lot of fat?
5. Do doctors warn people in your country that they eat too much fat? Too much sugar? Too much salt? Give examples of the foods that doctors warn people about.

G. DISCUSSION: *WITH YOUR CLASS*

Talk about Chart 2.3 with your teacher. Find out what the abbreviations *oz, tbsp, gm,* and *mg* mean. Then answer the following questions orally about the information in the chart.

1. How many milligrams of iron does one large apple supply?
2. How many calories are there in 3.2 ounces of beef?
3. How many milligrams of vitamin C does a medium orange contain?
4. How many grams of protein do 6 ounces of milk provide?
5. How many milligrams of calcium are there in one tablespoon of butter?
6. How many grams of protein does one cup of cooked rice have?

CHART 2.3

Food	Serving	Calories	(gm) Protein	(mg) Calcium	(mg) Iron	(IU) A	(mg) C	(IU) D
apple	1 large	117	0.6	12	0.6	180	9	0
banana	1	176	2.4	16	1.2	860	20	0
beef	3.2 oz	214	24.7	10	3.1	0	0	0
butter	1 tbsp	100	0.1	33	0.0	460	0	5
milk	6 oz	124	6.4	216	0.2	293	2	4
orange	1 medium	68	1.4	50	0.6	285	74	0
rice,cooked	1 cup	201	4.2	13	0.5	0	0	0

H.   WRITTEN PRACTICE: *ON YOUR OWN*

Use the information in Chart 2.3 to make sentences with the verbs *have, provide, supply,* or *contain*. Be sure to punctuate your sentences correctly. Follow the model.

<u>MODEL:</u>   one large apple / milligrams of calcium

One large apple contains 12 milligrams of calcium.

1. one medium orange / milligrams of calcium

2. one cup of cooked rice / grams of protein

3. twelve ounces of milk / calories

4. one tablespoon of butter / milligrams of iron

5. one large banana / milligrams of calcium

6. one serving of beef / calories

7. one large apple / milligrams of vitamin C

8. three tablespoons of butter / calories

9. one serving of beef / grams of protein

10. one medium orange / milligrams of iron

NUTRIENTS SUPPLIED BY COMMON FOOD

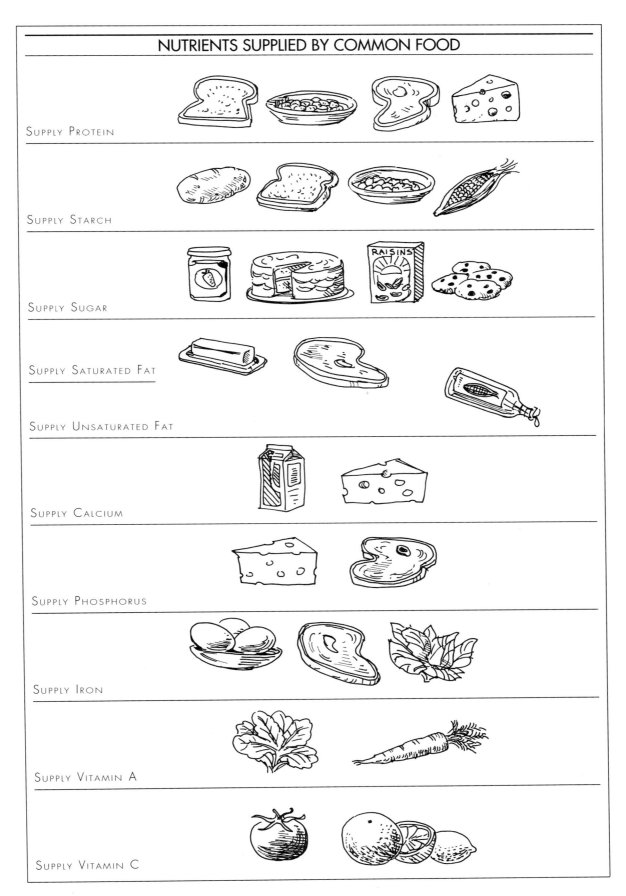

Supply Protein

Supply Starch

Supply Sugar

Supply Saturated Fat

Supply Unsaturated Fat

Supply Calcium

Supply Phosphorus

Supply Iron

Supply Vitamin A

Supply Vitamin C

Figure 2.5

I. ORAL PRACTICE: *WITH YOUR CLASS*

I.1. Answering Questions

Look at the pictures in the Figure 2.5. Answer these questions, based on the information in the chart.

1. What does bread supply?
2. Which kinds of food give the body saturated fat?
3. Which kinds of food supply both protein and starch?
4. Do vegetables provide protein?
5. Which nutrients does cheese have?
6. Which kinds of food contain sugar?
7. Do eggs supply iron?
8. What four nutrients does meat provide?
9. Is there phosphorous in cookies?
10. What kinds of vegetables contain vitamin A?

I.2. Answering Questions

Use the information in the Figure 2.5 and the information you learned about nutrients in Exercise D on page 43, to answer the following questions.

1. What kinds of food help to build strong bones?
2. What kinds of food are good for healthy blood?
3. What kinds of food does the body get energy from?
4. What kinds of food are important for making new cells?
5. What kinds of food does the body need for making enzymes?

J. ORAL PRACTICE: *IN PAIRS*

Take turns asking and answering these questions, which are based on all the information in this chapter. Partner A asks questions 1–7 while Partner B listens and answers. Then, Partner B asks questions 8–14 while Partner A listens and answers.

MODELS:

Partner A:	*Does chicken supply sugar?*
Partner B:	*No. Chicken doesn't supply sugar.*
	OR
	No, it doesn't.

Partner A:	*Do carrots contain vitamin A?*
Partner B:	*Yes. Carrots contain vitamin A.*
	OR
	Yes, they do.

1. Do apples contain a lot of protein?
2. Is bread a rich source of vitamin C?
3. Does milk provide calcium?
4. Is cauliflower a fruit?
5. Are nuts root vegetables?
6. Does meat contain protein?
7. Does meat have sugar in it?
8. Do vegetables contain a lot of fat?
9. Does the body burn carbohydrates for energy?
10. Is fruit a good source of carbohydrates?
11. Do potatoes grow on bushes?
12. Are dairy products a good source of calcium?
13. Does milk supply vitamin C?
14. Do babies need milk?

K. WRITTEN PRACTICE: *ON YOUR OWN*

Write a question for each group of words. Be sure to punctuate your sentences correctly. Follow the models.

MODELS: broccoli / supply / iron

Does broccoli supply iron?

what nutrients / milk / provide

What nutrients does milk provide?

1. cereal / give / protein

_____

2. what vitamin / tomatoes / provide

_____

3. meat / provide / iron

_____

4. what / corn / supply

_____

5. vegetables / contain / iron

_____

6. what nutrients / meat / provide

_____

7. what mineral / cheese / contain

_____

8. bread / have / starch

_____

9. oranges / supply / vitamin C

_____

10. what nutrients / dairy products / have

_____

L. ORAL PRACTICE: *In Pairs*

Interview your partner about what he or she typically eats for breakfast, lunch, and dinner, and snacks. Write the information in the chart below.

CHART 2.5

Breakfast	Lunch	Dinner	Snacks

M. WRITTEN PRACTICE: *In Pairs*

With your partner, look at the kinds of food that he or she usually eats. Identify the sources of the main nutrients in your partner's diet. Fill in the chart below with the information from Exercise L.

CHART 2.6

Protein	Fat	Carbohydrates	Vitamins Minerals

N. WRITTEN PRACTICE: *ON YOUR OWN*

Look at the information in the charts for Exercises L and M. Using that information, write ten sentences that describe the food in your partner's diet and the sources of nutrients.

MODELS: *Carlos eats toast for breakfast. Toast provides carbohydrates.*

Yoko has a hamburger for lunch. There is protein and fat in a

hamburger. The bun has carbohydrates.

Digestion
LESSON 3

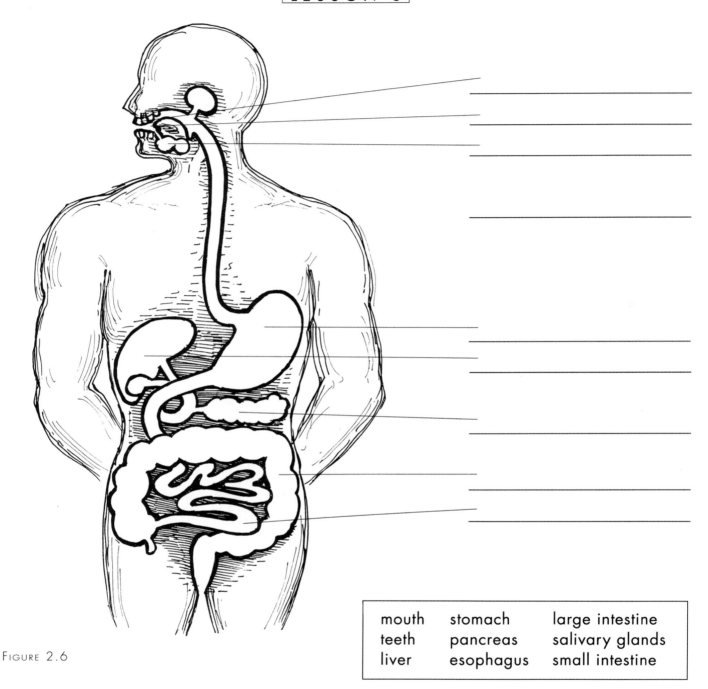

FIGURE 2.6

mouth	stomach	large intestine
teeth	pancreas	salivary glands
liver	esophagus	small intestine

A. WARM-UP: *WITH YOUR CLASS*

Look at the picture in Figure 2.6 with your teacher. Fill in the blanks with the words that you already know. Check your answers with your classmates' answers.

1. How many parts of the body help to digest food?
2. Where does digestion start?
3. Why are teeth important for digestion?
4. Why are the salivary glands important for digestion?
5. What does the stomach do?

B. FOCUS VOCABULARY: *ON YOUR OWN*

On the lines below, write down new words that you learn in class. Add to your list as you study about the digestive system. Focus on verbs, nouns, and adjectives.

_____   _____   _____

_____   _____   _____

_____   _____   _____

_____   _____   _____

_____   _____   _____

C. READING

Digestion

The human body receives the main nutrient groups — protein, fat, carbohydrates, vitamins, and minerals — from the food that it digests. When the body digests food, it breaks the food down into the nutrients that it needs.

The Mouth

The first step in the process of digestion takes place in the mouth. When people put food into their mouths, they use their teeth to chew it. When people chew their food, they break it up into small pieces which they can then swallow. The salivary glands are in the mouth. They produce saliva. Saliva makes the food moist and soft so that it is easier to chew.

The Esophagus

The second step in digestion takes place in the esophagus. When people swallow their food, it moves through the esophagus to the stomach. The esophagus is a large muscle which looks like a pipe.

The Stomach

The third step in the digestive process occurs in the stomach. The enzymes and digestive juices in the stomach break the food down into nutrients. For example, the stomach breaks down a piece of cheese into protein, fat, and vitamin A. The stomach is a powerful muscle. When it digests food, it contracts and expands. In this way, it continues to break the food up. The stomach can digest protein. The protein passes through the walls of the stomach into the blood stream. However, the stomach cannot digest the other nutrients: carbohydrates, fat, vitamins, or minerals.

The Small Intestine

Food stays in the stomach from two to five hours before the other nutrients pass into the small intestine. The fourth step in digestion is in the small intestine. The small intestine is very long, about twenty feet long for a human being. It finishes the digestion of the other nutrients: carbohydrates, fat, vitamins, and minerals. Then the thin walls of the small intestine absorb the nutrients, and they pass into the blood stream. The blood stream carries the nutrients to the body's cells.

The Large Intestine

The large intestine completes the process of digestion. It is five feet long in human beings. The large intestine removes the waste material that the body cannot digest and cannot use.

Fiber, for instance, is part of food, but the body cannot digest it. Fiber leaves the small intestine and moves into the large intestine. Then the large intestine takes it away.

The Pancreas and the Liver

There are two other important organs in digestion. The pancreas is an important organ because it produces enzymes which it sends to the small intestine. The liver is another important organ. It also produces enzymes which help the small intestine to digest food.

The human digestive system is very complicated. All of the digestive organs have their special functions to perform so that digestion can take place.

D. COMPREHENSION: *On Your Own and With Your Class*

D.1. True or False: *On Your Own*

Read each statement below about the digestive system and circle *True* or *False*. If the statement is false, correct it.

1. The pancreas produces saliva.   **True**   **False**

2. The small intestine is longer than the large intestine.   **True**   **False**

3. The stomach can digest all nutrients.   **True**   **False**

4. The last step in the digestive process is in the esophagus.   **True**   **False**

5. The human body cannot digest fiber.   **True**   **False**

6. The walls of the stomach absorb protein.   **True**   **False**

7. There are five main steps in the digestive process.   **True**   **False**

8. Digestion starts in the mouth.   **True**   **False**

9. The blood carries fiber to the body's cells.   **True**   **False**

10. The stomach breaks food down into nutrients.   **True**   **False**

D.2. Oral Practice: *With Your Class*

With your classmates, take turns asking and answering these questions, which are based on the reading about digestion.

1. Where does digestion begin?
2. What organs produce enzymes for digestion?
3. How long does food remain in the stomach?
4. How many nutrients can the stomach digest?
5. How long is the small intestine?
6. What organ expands and contracts?
7. What organ removes undigested material?
8. What function does saliva have?
9. What parts of the digestive system can absorb the nutrients?
10. Where does the blood stream carry the nutrients?
11. What do the salivary glands produce?
12. What breaks food up in the mouth?

E.   VOCABULARY PRACTICE: *ON YOUR OWN*

Use the following verbs or phrases to finish the sentences below. Use each verb or phrase only once. Change the form of the verb when necessary.

absorb	expand	provide
be like	make	remain
break down	move through	remove
carry	pass into	supply
chew	produce	swallow

1. The teeth _____ food in the mouth.

2. Saliva _____ the food soft and moist.

3. The esophagus _____ a long pipe.

4. The stomach _____ and contracts when it digests food.

5. The enzymes and digestive juices _____ food in the stomach.

6. Carbohydrates _____ fuel for the body.

7. Protein _____ building material for cells.

8. The walls of the small intestine _____ the nutrients into the blood stream.

9. The large intestine _____ fiber from the body.

10. The blood _____ nutrients to cells.

11. The nutrients _____ the small intestine when they leave the stomach.

12. The food _____ the esophagus to the stomach.

13. The food leaves the mouth when people _____ it.

14. The liver and the pancreas _____ enzymes.

15. Food _____ in the stomach for two to five hours.

F. ORAL PRACTICE: *IN PAIRS*

Work with a partner and follow these directions.

Partner A: Look only at Column A. Cover Column B with a piece of paper. Ask a question about the missing information in Column A.

Partner B: Look only at Column B. Cover Column A with a piece of paper. Answer the question with the information in Column B. Use a complete sentence.

MODEL: **Column A**   **Column B**

The stomach makes _____. (what)   enzymes
Partner A: *What does the stomach make?*
Partner B: *The stomach makes enzymes.*
                    OR
            It makes enzymes.

Column A	**Column B**
1. The human body needs _____. (what)	1. food
2. Food has _____. (what)	2. nutrients
3. The first step in digestion is _____. (where)	3. in the mouth
4. Teeth break up _____ in the mouth. (what)	4. food
5. There is saliva _____ (where)	5. in the mouth
6. Saliva makes _____ soft. (what)	6. food
7. The second step in digestion is _____. (where)	7. in the esophagus
8. The esophagus is _____. (what)	8. a large muscle
9. The esophagus carries _____. (what)	9. food
10. The stomach digests _____. (what)	10. protein

Now change roles with your partner.

Column A	**Column B**
1. The small intestine digests _____. (what)	1. carbohydrates and fat
2. The wall of the small intestine absorbs _____. (what)	2. nutrients
3. The last step of digestion is _____. (where)	3. in the large intestine
4. Fiber is _____ food. (what)	4. undigestible
5. The large intestine takes away _____. (what)	5. waste
6. The pancreas makes _____. (what)	6. enzymes
7. The pancreas sends enzymes _____. (where)	7. to the small intestine
8. The liver produces _____ for the small intestine. (what)	8. enzymes
9. The salivary glands produce _____. (what)	9. saliva
10. The body burns _____ for energy. (what)	10. carbohydrates

G. WRITTEN PRACTICE: *ON YOUR OWN*

Write a paragraph about the process of digestion. Remember to explain all the steps in the process. Write at least ten sentences. (The first sentence is done for you.) Here are some vocabulary words to help you.

esophagus	chew
stomach	swallow
small intestine	contrast
large intestine	expand
pancreas	absorb
liver	move through
saliva	pass into
enzyme	

Try to include some of these sequence expressions.

Next   Then   After that   Finally

The first step in the process of digestion is in the mouth. _____

_____

_____

_____

_____

_____

_____

_____

_____

_____

_____

_____

_____

_____

_____

_____

_____

Figure 3.1   Four Types of Climates

Weather and Climate

CHAPTER 3

What is Climate?

LESSON 1

A. WARM-UP: *IN SMALL GROUPS*

Look at the pictures in Figure 3.1 with the members of your group. What type of climate does each picture show? Discuss the questions below with your group and then talk about the answers with the whole class.

1. What are the people wearing?
2. What are the houses like?
3. What is the plant life like?
4. Can you guess what the temperature is?
5. What kind of weather is in the picture?

B. FOCUS VOCABULARY: *ON YOUR OWN*

On the lines below, write down new words that you learn in class. Add to your list as you study types of weather and climate. Focus on nouns and adjectives.

_____   _____   _____

_____   _____   _____

_____   _____   _____

_____   _____   _____

C. READING

What Is Climate?

Climate is a regular pattern of weather in an area over a long period of time. The weather conditions in an area can change often from day to day, but the climate stays the same from year to year. Scientists measure and record the temperature, moisture, and amount of sunlight in an area. With this information, they can divide the world into four general climate zones: tropical, arid, temperate, and polar.

Tropical Climate

A tropical climate is generally warm and wet. Tropical areas are located near the equator where they receive the sun's direct light all year. The temperature in a tropical area ranges from 68° F to 93° F (20° C to 34° C). The amount of rainfall per year is always at least 80 inches (200 cm). Thunderstorms occur often. There are more kinds of plants and animals

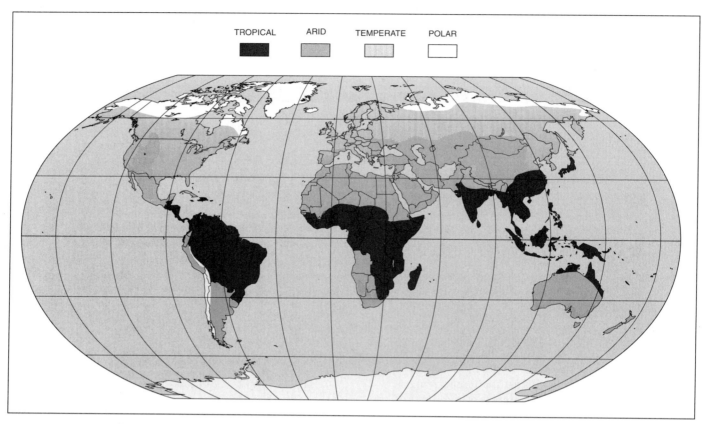

FIGURE 3.2   Climate Map of the World

in tropical areas than in any other climate zone. In tropical areas, where rainfall is heavy throughout the year, there are large rain forests. The largest tropical rain forests are in Brazil, in central Africa, and in Indonesia. In other tropical areas, there are two seasons every year, a wet season with heavy rainfall and a dry season.

Arid Climate

The arid areas of the world receive very little rainfall. Arid areas that get less than 10 in. (25 cm) of precipitation per year are called deserts. Sometimes there will be no precipitation at all in a desert for many years. Deserts occupy one-fifth of the earth's surface. The largest desert in the world is the Sahara, which is 3.5 million square miles (9 million square km). The temperature in the Sahara may reach 122° F (50° C) in the daytime, but it falls rapidly at night. Deserts which are not close to the equator, such as the Gobi Desert in Mongolia, are very cold in the winter. Not all deserts are sandy. In fact, only one-eighth of the world's deserts are sandy.

Temperate Climate

Temperate zones are located halfway between the equator and the North Pole or the South Pole. Temperate zones generally receive a great amount of direct sunlight in the summer months. However, they receive a much smaller amount of sunlight in the winter months. Temperatures in these areas range from around 100° F (58° C) in the summer to −10° F (−23° C) in the winter. There is regular precipitation in temperate areas throughout the year, with rainfall in the spring, summer, and autumn and snow in the winter. The southern temperate areas have little rainfall in the summer. The northern temperate areas have cold winters and heavy snowfall.

Polar Climate

Polar climates are mainly in the Arctic around the North Pole and in Antarctica around the South Pole. These regions have very cold temperatures and very little rainfall. There are only two regular seasons: summer and winter. The summers are short and cool. The average summer temperature usually does not go higher than 50° F (10° C). The winters are long and cold, and last around nine months. The temperature in the winter is frequently –76° F (–60° C). Trees do not grow in polar areas. In the summer, only a little grass and some flowers grow.

D. COMPREHENSION: *ON YOUR OWN*

D.1. True or False

Read each statement below about climates and circle *True* or *False*. If the statement is false, correct it.

1. Tropical climate zones are located near the equator.   **True**   **False**

_____

2. The climate in an area often changes.   **True**   **False**

_____

3. A temperate climate has precipitation all year.   **True**   **False**

_____

4. It often rains in arid climate zones.   **True**   **False**

_____

5. Forests cover most of the polar climate zones.   **True**   **False**

_____

6. The temperature is sometimes below 32° F (0° C) in temperate climate zones. **True**   **False**

_____

7. There is a long winter in tropical climate zones.   **True**   **False**

_____

8. The earth's surface is 20 percent desert.   **True**   **False**

_____

9. Most deserts are not sandy.   **True**   **False**

_____

10. Polar climates exist only in the Arctic and the Antarctic.   **True**   **False**

_____

D.2. Comprehension Questions

Answer the following questions about the reading. Write a complete sentence to answer each question.

1. How many general climate zones are there?

_____

2. What information do scientists need to study climate zones?

_____

3. How much rain is there every year in tropical climate zones?

_____

4. How big is the Sahara Desert?

_____

5. When is the temperature hot in a temperate climate zone?

_____

6. How many seasons are there in the polar climate zones?

_____

E. DISCUSSION: *WITH YOUR CLASS*

Discuss these questions with your classmates. Take turns asking and answering questions.

1. What are some countries that have typical tropical climates?
2. What are some countries that have typical temperate climates?
3. What other deserts do you know besides the Sahara?
4. What is the climate of your country?
5. Is there more than one climate zone in your country?
6. How many seasons are there in your climate zone?
7. Is the climate in the United States different from the climate in your country?
8. How does the climate in your country affect the way that people live? For example, how does it affect clothing, houses, buildings, food, and so forth?

F. ORAL PRACTICE: *IN PAIRS*

Look at the climate map on page 60. Then ask questions, using the words below. Find the answers on the map or in the reading. Student A asks questions for 1–8; then student B asks questions for 9–16. Follow the model.

__MODEL:__   which / African country / have / an arid climate
         Partner A: *Which African country has an arid climate?*
         Partner B: *Egypt has an arid climate.*

1. which / Asian country / have / a temperate climate
2. how many / climate zones / Russia / have
3. what kind / climate / Venezuela / have
4. how many / seasons / Iceland / have

5. which climate zone / have / very long winter
6. which climate / have / a lot of rainfall
7. where / the sun / shine / twelve hours every day
8. when / it / snow / in Asia
9. how many climate zones / be / there / in the United States
10. which climate zone / have / very short summer
11. what kind / climate / Hawaii / have
12. which climate zone / be / Europe / in
13. where / it / rain / very often
14. when / the temperature / be / low / in the desert
15. which kind / climate / have / four seasons
16. how many months / last / summer / in the Arctic

TABLE 3.1   Study the patterns for **comparing short adjectives.**

cool / hot					
Canada	has a	**cooler**	climate than	Venezuela	(has).
Brazil		**hotter**		Alaska	
OR					
Canada	is	**cooler**	than	Venezuela	(is).
Brazil		**hotter**		Alaska	

G.   ORAL PRACTICE: *IN PAIRS*

G.1. Asking and Answering Questions

Ask questions, using the words below. Find answers by looking at the information on the climate map on page 60 and in the reading. Follow the models and the patterns in Table 3.1.

MODELS: climate / cool / Venezuela / Canada?   Why?

         Partner A: *Which country has a cooler climate, Venezuela or Canada?*
         Partner B: *Canada has a cooler climate.*

         Partner A: *Why is the climate cooler in Canada?*
         Partner B: *Because Canada is in a temperate zone.*

1. temperature / hot / Brazil / Alaska?   Why?
2. climate / dry / Tunisia / Thailand?   Why?
3. weather / cool / Taiwan / Korea?   Why?
4. winter / long / France / Canada?   Why?
5. summer days / long / United States / Zaire?   Why?
6. winters / cold / Sweden / Japan?   Why?
7. the climate / wet / Great Britain / Antarctica?   Why?
8. the desert / large / Australia / North Africa?   Why?
9. the temperature at night / low / India / Egypt?   Why?
10. summers / short / Greenland / Mexico?   Why?

TABLE 3.2   Study the patterns for **comparing long adjectives.**

> The weather in Zaire is **more tropical** than the weather in Panama is.
>
> The weather in France is **more temperate** than the weather in Iceland is.

G.2. Asking and Answering Questions

Answer the following questions, which are based on the map and the reading. You may also use your own opinion. Follow the models and the patterns in Table 3.2.

MODELS   climate / comfortable / Egypt / France?   Why?

Partner A: *Where is the climate more comfortable, in Egypt or in France?*
Partner B: *The climate is more comfortable in France.*

Partner A: *Why is the climate more comfortable in France?*
Partner B: *Because it is very hot in Egypt.*

1. climate / comfortable / Mexico / Canada?   Why?
2. weather / pleasant / Hawaii / Korea?   Why?
3. seasons / interesting / Japan / Antarctica?   Why?
4. precipitation / regular / Saudi Arabia / Germany?   Why?
5. climate / tropical / Ecuador / India?   Why?
6. seasons / variable / Thailand / Russia?   Why?
7. rainfall / frequent / Greenland / Indonesia?   Why?
8. plants / beautiful / Antarctica / Brazil?   Why?
9. weather conditions / difficult / Spain / Iceland?   Why?
10. climate / temperate / Norway / Great Britain?   Why?

TABLE 3.3   Study the patterns for **comparing nouns.**

noncountable noun	Brazil	has	**more**	rainfall	than	Saudi Arabia has.
	Saudi Arabia		**less**			Brazil has.
countable noun	Australia	has	**more**	climate zones	than	Greece has.
	Greece		**fewer**			Australia has.

G.3. Asking and Answering Questions

Answer the following questions which are based on the information on the map and in the reading. Follow the models and the patterns in Table 3.3.

MODELS: more rainfall / Malaysia / Germany?   Why?

Partner A: *Which country has more rainfall, Malaysia or Germany?*
Partner B: *Malaysia has more rainfall.*
    OR
    Malaysia does.

Partner A: Why does Malaysia have more rainfall than Germany?
Partner B: Because Malaysia has a tropical climate.

1. more rainfall / Zaire / Morocco?   Why?
2. more sunlight / Ecuador / Norway?   Why?

3. more summer days / Iceland / the United States?   Why?
4. more seasons / Japan / Indonesia?   Why?
5. less sunlight / Antarctica / the Middle East?   Why?
6. less rainfall / Egypt / Thailand?   Why?
7. fewer winter days / Canada / Panama?   Why?
8. fewer seasons / Central America / North America?   Why?
9. less snow / Norway / Italy?   Why?
10. fewer climate zones / Australia / India?   Why?

CHART 3.1

		TEMPERATURE				PRECIPITATION	
		average daily				average monthly	
		F		C		in.	mm.
		max	min	max	min		
TROPICAL							
Kinshasa	Jan	87	70	31	21	5.3	135
	Jul	81	64	27	18	0.1	3
Rio de Janeiro	Jan	86	77	30	25	2.1	53
	Jul	80	71	27	22	10	254
Bangkok	Jan	89	68	32	20	0.3	8
	Jul	90	76	32	24	6.3	160
TEMPERATE							
Santiago	Jan	85	53	29	12	0.1	3
	Jul	59	37	15	3	3	76
Beijing	Jan	34	14	1	-10	0.2	4
	Jul	87	69	31	21	7.2	183
Tokyo	Jan	47	29	8	-2	1.9	48
	Jul	83	70	28	21	5.6	142
Moscow	Jan	15	3	-9	-16	1.5	39
	Jul	73	55	23	13	3.5	88
London	Jan	43	36	6	2	2.1	54
	Jul	71	56	22	14	2.2	57
Ottawa	Jan	21	3	-6	-16	2.9	74
	Jul	81	58	27	14	3.4	86
Washington	Jan	42	27	6	-3	3.4	86
	Jul	87	68	31	20	4.4	112
ARID							
Riyadh	Jan	70	46	21	8	0.1	3
	Jul	107	78	42	26	0	0
Cairo	Jan	65	47	18	8	0.2	5
	Jul	96	70	36	21	0	0

H. WRITTEN PRACTICE: *ON YOUR OWN*

Look at Chart 3.1, which shows average temperature and precipitation for twelve cities in the world. Then, write a question, using the cue words below. Write a short answer based on the information in the chart.

MODEL: have / high / average temperature / Tokyo / Moscow?

Which city has a higher average temperature, Tokyo or Moscow?

Tokyo does.

1. have / high / average temperature / Beijing / Bangkok?

_____

_____

2. have / low / average temperature / London / Kinshasa?

_____

_____

3. receive / less / precipitation / Rio de Janeiro / Riyadh?

_____

_____

4. receive / more / precipitation / Ottawa / Washington, D.C.?

_____

_____

5. have / many / hot days / Cairo / Santiago?

_____

_____

6. have / few / hot days / Bangkok / Moscow?

_____

_____

7. have / many / dry days / Kinshasa / Washington, D.C.?

_____

_____

8. have / wet weather / in July / Santiago / Rio de Janeiro?

_____

_____

9. have / cold weather / in January / Moscow / Ottawa?

_____

_____

10. receive / a little sunshine / in July / London / Tokyo?

_____

_____

I. DISCUSSION: *WITH YOUR CLASS*

Talk with your classmates about the climate in the area where you are living now. With your teacher, make a list of factors that affect your climate. Some of the factors that affect the climate and the weather in an area include high mountains, the ocean, the wind, and altitude. What do you think is important for the climate and the weather of the area where you are living now?

J. FOCUS VOCABULARY: *ON YOUR OWN*

On the lines below, write down any words that you learn while you are discussing the factors that affect climate. Focus on nouns, verbs, and adjectives.

_____	_____	_____
_____	_____	_____
_____	_____	_____
_____	_____	_____
_____	_____	_____

K. READING AND LISTENING: *ON YOUR OWN AND WITH YOUR CLASS*

First, read the following paragraph. Then listen to your teacher, who will give you more information about factors that affect climate. Take notes while your teacher is talking. Write down the important facts in the chart below. When you have completed your chart, compare your information with your classmates' information.

Temperature and Precipitation

Scientists define climate on the basis of two things: temperature and precipitation. Precipitation includes rain, snow, hail, fog, and other forms of moisture. Many factors can affect temperature and precipitation. Two places that are in the same climate zone can have very different weather patterns because of these factors.

Factors That Affect Temperature and Precipitation

CHART 3.2

Factors That Affect Temperature	Factors That Affect Precipitation

L.   ORAL AND WRITTEN PRACTICE: *IN PAIRS*

L.1. Discussing Temperature and Precipitation

Look at the factors in Chart 3.2 that affect temperature and precipitation. Explain to your partner which factors are important for the temperature and precipitation in your country. Take notes on Chart 3.3 as you listen to your partner talk about the factors that affect temperature and precipitation in his or her country.

CHART 3.3

Your Country	Your Partner's Country

L.2. Writing about Temperature and Precipitation in Your Country

Write a paragraph with five or more sentences to explain which factors affect the temperature and precipitation in your country.

_____

_____

_____

_____

_____

L.3. Writing about Temperature and Precipitation in Your Partner's Country

Write a paragraph with five or more sentences to explain which factors affect the temperature and precipitation in your partner's country.

_____

_____

_____

_____

_____

_____

_____

_____

_____

_____

TABLE 3.4   Study the patterns for talking about **actions that are continuous**.

It	**is**	**raining**	in	Houston	today.	
	isn't			Los Angeles		
Is	it	**raining**	in	Houston	today?	Yes, it **is**.
				Los Angeles		No, it **isn't**.

FIGURE 3.3 Weather Map of the United States

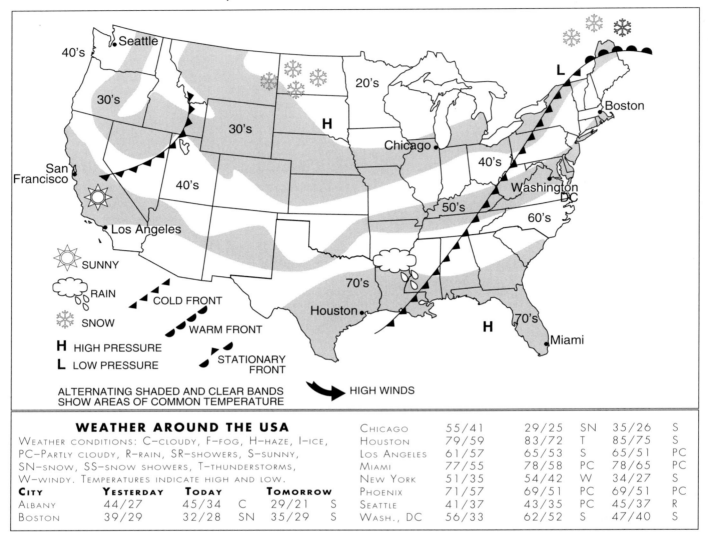

WEATHER AROUND THE USA

WEATHER CONDITIONS: C–CLOUDY, F–FOG, H–HAZE, I–ICE,
PC–PARTLY CLOUDY, R–RAIN, SR–SHOWERS, S–SUNNY,
SN–SNOW, SS–SNOW SHOWERS, T–THUNDERSTORMS,
W–WINDY. TEMPERATURES INDICATE HIGH AND LOW.

CITY	YESTERDAY	TODAY		TOMORROW	
ALBANY	44/27	45/34	C	29/21	S
BOSTON	39/29	32/28	SN	35/29	S
CHICAGO	55/41	29/25	SN	35/26	S
HOUSTON	79/59	83/72	T	85/75	S
LOS ANGELES	61/57	65/53	S	65/51	PC
MIAMI	77/55	78/58	PC	78/65	PC
NEW YORK	51/35	54/42	W	34/27	S
PHOENIX	71/57	69/51	PC	69/51	PC
SEATTLE	41/37	43/35	PC	45/37	R
WASH., DC	56/33	62/52	S	47/40	S

M. ORAL PRACTICE: *In Pairs*

Talk about the weather map of the continental United States, above, with your teacher. Discuss the weather symbols. Then, ask and answer questions with your partner, using the information in column A, below. Use the weather map and the suggestions in column B for your answers. Follow the models and the patterns in Table 3.4.

M.1. Where Is It Raining Today?

MODEL: where / it / rain / today
   Partner A: *Where is it raining today?*
   Partner B: *It is raining in Houston today.*

Column A	Column B
1. where / it / rain / today	Houston
2. where / the sun / shine / today	Los Angeles
3. where / it / snow / today	Boston
4. where / it / freeze / today	Chicago
5. where / it / thunder / today	Houston
6. where / the wind / blow / today	New York

M.2. Where Is It Windy Today?

MODEL: where / it / windy / today?
  Partner A: *Where is it windy today?*
  Partner B: *It is windy in New York today.*

Column A
1. where / it / foggy / today?
2. where / it / cloudy / today?
3. where / it / rainy / today?
4. where / it / sunny / today?
5. where / it / chilly / today?
6. where / it / breezy / today?
7. where / it / muggy / today?
8. where / it / icy / today?

Column B
San Francisco
Boston
Houston
Los Angeles
Washington, D.C.
Seattle
Miami
Chicago

FIGURE 3.4   **Different Seasons**

N. WRITTEN PRACTICE: *ON YOUR OWN*

Look at the pictures in Figure 3.4 about weather in four different seasons. Use the words below to write a sentence about what is happening in the pictures.

MODEL: the wind / blow

The wind is blowing.

Winter

1. snow / fall

2. children / play / snow

3. man / shovel / snow

Spring

1. flowers / bloom

2. people / plant / seeds / in their gardens

3. children / fly / kites

Summer

1. people / swim

2. people / have / picnics

3. the crops / grow / in the fields

Autumn

1. the leaves / fall / from the trees

2. people / wear / sweaters

3. farmers / harvest / crops

Unusual Weather

LESSON 2

FIGURE 3.5   Types of Unusual Weather

A.   WARM-UP: *WITH YOUR CLASS*

Discuss the pictures with your classmates. With your teacher, fill in the blanks for each picture.
What kind of unusual weather is there in the area where you are living now? What kind of unusual
weather is there in your country?

B.   FOCUS VOCABULARY: *ON YOUR OWN*

On the lines below, write the new words that you learn in class. Add to the list as you study unusual
weather conditions. Focus on nouns and verbs.

_____   _____   _____

_____   _____   _____

_____   _____   _____

_____   _____   _____

_____   _____   _____

_____   _____   _____

Unusual Weather

Lightning

When the wind carries small drops of water up and down very quickly inside a cloud, electricity is made at the top and the bottom of that cloud. When the electricity from the top of the cloud meets the electricity from the bottom, it creates a spark. That spark is a flash of lightning. The lightning flash is as hot as 50,000° F (27,760° C). Every year lightning causes many fires and kills people and animals.

Thunder

Thunder is the rumbling sound that is made by lightning. The air around a lightning flash becomes very hot. The heated air then moves so quickly that it makes a noise like a bang. The rumbling sound that people hear is the echo of that bang.

Sound travels one mile in five seconds. Here is a simple way to know how far away the lightning and thunder are: When you see the lightning flash, start to count slowly. When you hear the thunder, stop counting. Divide the number by five; the answer is the number of miles away that the storm is.

Tornadoes

A tornado is a storm that concentrates a great deal of energy into a small space. When hot and cold air pass each other in opposite directions, they get locked together and the air begins to spin. During a tornado, the wind spins around very fast and forms a funnel. This funnel sucks up everything in its path, like a vacuum cleaner does. The funnel-shaped cloud twists and bends as it moves, so it is often called a twister. The twisting wind inside the funnel moves as fast as 200 miles (320 km) per hour.

Hurricanes and Typhoons

A hurricane, or typhoon, is a large storm that starts over the ocean in warm weather. When the storm starts over the Atlantic Ocean, it is called a hurricane. Storms that start over the Pacific Ocean are called typhoons. These storms form in tropical climate zones in the summer or autumn. The warm water from the ocean evaporates into the air. When the warm air rises high into the sky, cool air rushes in to replace it. This creates a spinning action that causes very strong winds. In the center, or eye, of the hurricane, there is no wind, but around the eye, winds move from 75 miles (120 km) to 200 miles (320 km) per hour. Hurricanes can be 600 miles (965 km) in diameter. They often bring heavy rain.

Blizzards

A blizzard is a storm that combines intense wind, cold temperature, and unusually heavy snowfall. The winds blow at least 35 miles (55 km) per hour, and the temperature is always below 20° F (–7° C). A blizzard occurs when a mass of cold air moves out of the Arctic and enters the temperate zone. During a blizzard, people outside or in cars cannot see anything, and they can die from the cold temperature if they do not find shelter. The snow in a blizzard is like powder, and it can also kill people if it goes into their lungs. During a blizzard in New York City in 1978, 14 inches (350 mm) of snow fell in 24 hours.

Hailstorms

Hailstorms occur most frequently during spring and summer in temperate climates.

Hailstones are frozen raindrops that form when strong wind pushes the raindrops high in the clouds, where the temperature is much colder. When the frozen raindrops start to fall, they are pushed up again to where they become bigger with more ice layers. Finally, the raindrops are too heavy to stay in the air, and they fall to earth as hail. Most hailstones are only as big as small peas, but occasionally they can be as big as baseballs. Hail can cause much damage to crops, trees, windows, cars, and airplanes. Large hailstones can kill animals and people.

D.   COMPREHENSION: *ON YOUR OWN*

D.1. True or False

Read each statement about unusual weather conditions and circle *True* or *False*. If the statement is false, correct it.

1. Thunder occurs before lightning.   **True**   **False**

_____

2. A tornado cloud is shaped like a funnel.   **True**   **False**

_____

3. Lightning is an electric spark.   **True**   **False**

_____

4. The eye of the hurricane is not windy.   **True**   **False**

_____

5. Sound moves one mile in five seconds.   **True**   **False**

_____

6. Blizzards start over warm ocean water.   **True**   **False**

_____

7. A tornado brings heavy snowfall.   **True**   **False**

_____

8. Hurricanes usually occur in the summer and in the autumn.   **True**   **False**

_____

9. Hailstorms cause much damage to farms.   **True**   **False**

_____

10. It is difficult to see during a blizzard.   **True**   **False**

_____

D.2. Comprehension Questions

Answer the following questions with information from the reading. Write a complete sentence for each question.

1. How does electricity form in a cloud?

_____

2. How can you know how far away lightning is?

3. Why is a tornado funnel cloud similar to a vacuum cleaner?

4. Why do hurricanes occur only in warm weather?

5. Where do blizzards come from?

6. Why do hailstones have many layers of ice?

E. DISCUSSION: *WITH YOUR CLASS*

Take turns with your classmates asking and answering these questions.

1. Which kinds of storms occur in your country's climate? Which ones never occur in your country's climate?
2. Why are storms dangerous? What are the effects of a bad storm?
3. What other kinds of bad weather conditions can you name? What causes them?

TABLE 3.5   Study the patterns for using **can**.

Lightning	**can**	cause	fires.	
Hurricanes	**cannot** **can't**	occur	in cold weather.	
Can lightning	cause	fires?		Yes, it **can**.
Can hurricanes	occur	in cold weather?		No, they **cannot**. No, they **can't**.

F. ORAL PRACTICE: *IN PAIRS*

Ask questions and give short answers using the patterns for *can*. Use the information in the reading to decide how to answer the questions. Follow the models and the patterns in Table 3.5.

MODELS: lightning / cause fires
               Partner A: *Can lightning cause fires?*
               Partner B: *Yes, it can.*

               hurricanes / occur / in cold weather
               Partner A: *Can hurricanes occur in cold weather?*
               Partner B: *No, they cannot.*

1. lightning / strike / a house
2. people / hear / thunder
3. sound / travel / quickly
4. thunder / cause / fires
5. a tornado / bring / snow

6. hailstones / damage / crops
7. blizzards / occur / in the summer
8. tornadoes / pick up / cars
9. a hailstone / be / large
10. hurricanes / start / in the Arctic

G. WRITTEN PRACTICE: *ON YOUR OWN*

Write questions with the following words. Answer the questions with information from the reading. Use *can* in your questions and in your answers. Follow the model. Check your answers with your class. Be sure to punctuate your sentences correctly.

MODEL: how fast / a hurricane / move

How fast can a hurricane move?

It can move 75 to 200 miles per hour.

1. how fast / a tornado / move

_____

_____

2. where / a hurricane / start

_____

_____

3. what / a funnel cloud / suck up

_____

_____

4. how fast / the sound of thunder / travel

_____

_____

5. what / people / see / during a blizzard

_____

_____

6. what / hailstorms / damage

_____

_____

7. how cold / the temperature / be / during a blizzard

_____

_____

8. how much snow / a blizzard / bring

_____

_____

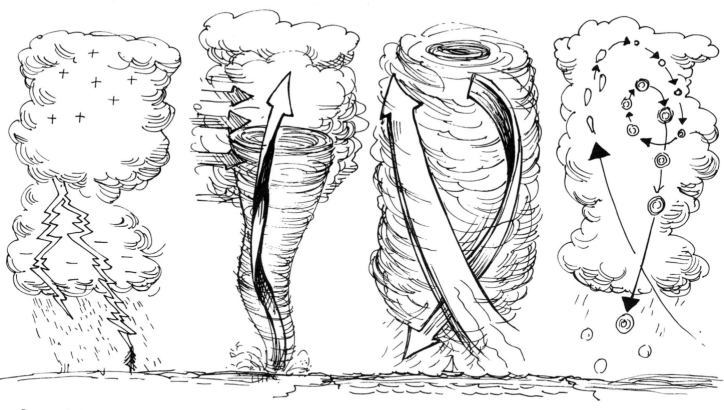

FIGURE 3.6

H. WRITTEN PRACTICE: *IN SMALL GROUPS*

Use the words below to make sentences about what is happening in the pictures of unusual weather. Take turns repeating the sentences orally. When you finish, decide how to put the sentences in order according to the first step, second step, third step, and so forth. Then, on the lines provided, write the sentences in the order that your group decides is correct. Use correct punctuation.

Thunder and Lightning

1. electricity / form / in a cloud
2. the sound / travel / one mile / in five seconds
3. air / become / hot / around the flash
4. water drops / move / up and down / in the cloud
5. electricity / create / a spark
6. the heated air / make / a bang

_____

_____

_____

_____

_____

_____

Tornadoes

1. hot and cold air / pass / each other
2. the funnel cloud / suck up / everything / on the ground
3. the air / spin around / very fast
4. the air / begin / to spin
5. the air / form / a funnel cloud
6. the funnel cloud / twist and bend

_____

_____

_____

_____

_____

Hurricanes

1. the cooler air / rush in
2. the warm air and the cool air / meet and spin
3. warm water in the ocean / evaporate / into the air
4. the warm air / rise / high into the sky
5. the cool air / replace / the warm air close to the ocean's surface
6. the wind / not blow / in the eye of the hurricane

_____

_____

_____

_____

_____

Blizzards

1. people / not go / outside
2. the wind / blow / very hard
3. the cold wind / enter / the temperate climate zone
4. a cold wind / come / from the Arctic region
5. it / bring / heavy snowfall
6. a lot of snow / fall

_____

_____

_____

_____

_____

Hailstorms

1. the raindrops / turn into / ice
2. a strong wind / push / the raindrops / high in the cloud
3. the frozen raindrops / collect / more layers of ice
4. raindrops / form / in the cloud
5. the wind / lift / the frozen raindrops / again and again
6. the hailstones / become / heavy / and / fall

_____

_____

_____

_____

_____

_____

FIGURE 3.7

I. WRITTEN PRACTICE: _IN PAIRS AND ON YOUR OWN_

Look at the picture above of flood conditions. With your partner, talk about what is happening in the pictures. Then, on your own, write sentences on the lines below about what is happening.

1. _____

2. _____

3. _____

4. _____

5. _____

The Greenhouse Effect

FIGURE 3.8

A. WARM-UP: *WITH YOUR CLASS*

Talk about the picture with your teacher. Discuss these questions: What is happening to the earth?
What is happening to the atmosphere? What is causing the problem? With your teacher and your
class, make a list of all the things that you know can cause pollution of the atmosphere.

_____

_____

_____

_____

_____

_____

_____

_____

_____

B. FOCUS VOCABULARY: *ON YOUR OWN*

On the lines below, write the new words that you learn in class. Add to your list as you study about the greenhouse effect. Focus on nouns and verbs.

_____ _____ _____

_____ _____ _____

_____ _____ _____

_____ _____ _____

C. READING *The Greenhouse Effect*

Did you know that the temperature of the earth's atmosphere is changing? The average temperature everywhere in the world is getting higher. Scientists are studying the rise in temperature because it is affecting weather and climate all around the world. This change in the earth's temperature is called the greenhouse effect.

Gases Polluting Atmosphere

Why are conditions in the earth's atmosphere changing? The most important reason is that pollution of the atmosphere from gases is increasing. There are three principal sources of this pollution. One source is the amount of carbon dioxide (CO_2) that comes from fossil fuels. People are burning more and more fossil fuels, such as coal, gas, and oil, to make energy for their homes, for transportation, and for industry. These fuels are releasing a great deal of CO_2 into the atmosphere.

Another source of pollution is chlorofluorocarbons (CFCs), which are increasing in the atmosphere. When people use spray cans, air conditioners, and refrigerators, they are adding to the amount of CFCs in the atmosphere.

A third source of atmospheric pollution is the amount of nitrous oxides (nitrogen and oxygen) in the air. Nitrous oxides are increasing because people are using artificial fertilizers for agriculture, destroying the tropical rain forests by fire, and burning fossil fuels.

Pollution Creating Greenhouse Effect

Carbon dioxide, chlorofluorocarbons, nitrous oxide, and other gases are polluting the earth's atmosphere. They are creating the greenhouse effect which is causing the earth's temperature to rise. The pollution is staying close to the surface of the earth. The heat from the sun is coming through the atmosphere to the earth, but it is not escaping because the pollution is keeping the heat close to the earth's surface. Like in a real greenhouse, the sun's heat can come into the atmosphere but it cannot go out again.

Warmer Temperatures Producing Negative Effects

Scientists are warning us that the greenhouse effect is going to change the earth's climates. The average world temperature is already warmer than it was in 1900. The greenhouse effect may make the average temperature 3° F to 9° F higher before the year 2030.

The amount of precipitation is already changing in many areas of the world. Some areas are getting drier. Droughts are occurring more frequently and lasting longer. In other areas the climate is getting wetter and there is more danger of floods.

The level of the oceans is getting higher. The warmer temperatures are causing the water in the oceans to expand. As a result, sea level is rising. Before the year 2030, the oceans are going to be 12 inches (30 cm) higher than they are now. Scientists are also predicting that if the earth's average temperature rises 9° F, the ice in Antarctica is going to melt and the oceans are going to rise 16 feet (4.5 meters) or more. Low land near the coasts is going to be under water.

Scientists Looking for Ways to Reduce the Greenhouse Effect

The greenhouse effect is a serious problem. It is already affecting the Earth. Scientists are discussing several ways to reduce the greenhouse effect. We must decrease the pollution in the atmosphere. Right now, industries, cars, airplanes, and houses are releasing 5.5 billion tons of CO_2 into the air every year. First, we must find cleaner fuels, such as solar energy or wind energy. Second, we must try to save energy. We are using too much electricity and too much fossil fuel. Cars and airplanes must become more efficient. It is going to be possible to go 100 miles with one gallon of gas in the future. Third, we must recycle more materials. People are wasting materials which can be used again. Finally, we must protect the rain forests. Trees are taking away 50 percent of the CO_2 in the air now, but there are not enough trees to protect us from the greenhouse effect. People are burning large areas of tropical rain forests now. This is destroying the world's green areas and releasing more CO_2 into the atmosphere.

D.   Written Practice: *In Pairs*

Work with your partner to complete the following outline about the information in the reading.

I.   **Gases are polluting the atmosphere.**

There are three main sources of atmospheric pollution.

A.   _____

Reason: _____

_____

B.   The amount of CFCs is increasing.

Reason: _____

_____

C.   _____

Reason: People are using artificial fertilizers, destroying rain forests, and burning fossil fuels.

II. **Pollution is creating the greenhouse effect.**

Pollution is creating a greenhouse for the earth.

A.   _____

B. The heat from the sun is coming through the atmosphere.

C. _____

D. The heat is staying close to the earth.

E. _____

III. **Warmer temperatures are producing negative effects.**

    A. The greenhouse effect is changing the earth's climates.

        1. _____

        2. The temperature is going to be 3° F to 9°F higher in 2030.

    B. Precipitation is changing.

        1. _____

        Example: Droughts are occurring more frequently.

        2. _____

        Example: _____

    C. _____

        1. The water in the oceans is expanding.

        Result: _____

        2. _____

        Result: The oceans are going to rise 16 feet.

IV. **Scientists are looking for ways to reduce the greenhouse effect.**

We must reduce pollution in the atmosphere.

    A. _____

    Example: We can use solar energy or wind energy.

    B. _____

    Example: We are using too much electricity and fossil fuel.

Example: _____

C. We must recycle more materials.

Example: _____

D. _____

Reason: Trees take away CO_2 from the atmosphere.

Danger: _____

E. DISCUSSION: *WITH YOUR CLASS*

Discuss these questions with your classmates.

1. What are five main ways that people are polluting the earth's atmosphere?
2. Scientists say that planting more trees will help to slow down the greenhouse effect. Why will this help?
3. Many of the world's large forests are being cut down. Why is this dangerous?
4. What can people do to reduce pollution in the atmosphere? What are some things that we can change in our daily lives?
5. What do you think the government should do?

TABLE 3.6   **Study the patterns for using better and worse.**

good/better	Solar energy is better than fossil fuels.
bad/worse	Pollution from industries is worse than pollution from agriculture.

F. ORAL PRACTICE: *WITH YOUR CLASS*

Discuss the following questions with your class. Answer each question based on the information in the reading or use your own opinion to give an answer. Use *better* or *worse* in your answers. Explain your answers to your classmates. Follow the model and the patterns in Table 3.6.

MODEL: Which source of pollution is worse, cars or spray cans?
           I think pollution from cars is worse than pollution from spray cans.

1. What is a better source of energy, solar energy or wind energy?
2. What is a better way to reduce pollution, find new fuels or use less energy?
3. Which kind of pollution is worse, water pollution or air pollution?
4. What is worse for the environment, coal or wood?
5. What is a worse problem, droughts or floods?
6. What is a better way to reduce CO_2 in the atmosphere, saving the rain forests or recycling materials?
7. Is an increase in the average world temperature better or worse for the environment?
8. Scientists are developing cars that use less gas. Is a fuel-efficient car better or worse than an electric car?

G.   WRITTEN PRACTICE: *ON YOUR OWN*

Write a question to find the missing word or words. Then write a complete sentence with the answer.

MODEL: Trees take _____ from the air.

  Q: *What do trees take from the air?*

  (CO_2)

  A: *They take CO_2 from the air.*

1. Scientists are studying _____.

   Q: _____
   (the greenhouse effect)

   A: _____

2. _____ is affecting the weather everywhere.

   Q: _____
   (the rise in temperature)

   A: _____

3. People burn _____ for energy.

   Q: _____
   (fuel)

   A: _____

4. Industries are releasing _____ into the atmosphere.

   Q: _____
   (a great deal of CO_2)

   A: _____

5. CFCs come from _____.

   Q: _____
   (spray cans)

   A: _____

6. _____ put nitrous oxide into the atmosphere.

   Q: _____
   (cars)

   A: _____

7. People are polluting _____ more and more.

   Q: _____
   (the atmosphere)

   A: _____

8. The pollution is staying _____.

   Q: _____
   (in the atmosphere)

   A: _____

9. _____ is absorbing the sun's heat.

   Q: _____
   (the pollution in the air)

   A: _____

10. Governments are trying to reduce _____.

    Q: _____
    (pollution)

    A: _____

H. WRITTEN PRACTICE: *ON YOUR OWN*

Finish each sentence on the right by putting the verb on the left into the blank. Pay attention to the tense. Follow the models.

MODELS: *affect:*   People _are affecting_ the earth's temperature now.

           reduce: Trees __reduce__ the amount of CO_2 in the air.

1. change   The climate _____ four times a year in a temperate climate zone.

2. change   The greenhouse effect _____ the climate now.

3. warm up   The earth _____ every year in the spring.

4. get warmer   The average temperature _____ now.

5. study   Scientists often _____ weather conditions.

6. cause   Industries _____ pollution now.

7. use   People _____ gas and electricity every day in their homes.

8. not rain   It _____ enough now in many areas.

9. cut down   People _____ the rain forests now.

10. release   Spray cans _____ CFCs into the air.

I.   ORAL PRACTICE: *IN PAIRS*

Interview your partner about pollution in his or her country. Ask questions, using the words below.
Pay attention to tense. Use the lines below to take notes on your partner's answers.

MODEL: your city / big
         Is your city big?

1. cars / produce / smog / now / in your city
2. what / people / in your city / do / with garbage
3. your government / make / laws / to reduce pollution / now
4. your country / be / near the ocean
5. ocean / polluted
6. rivers / in your country / clean
7. people / in your country / use / solar energy
8. companies / in your country / cut down / forests
9. farmers / use / chemicals / on their crops / in your country
10. people / in your country / use / less plastic / now

_____

_____

_____

_____

J.   WRITTEN PRACTICE: *ON YOUR OWN*

Use the information from your interview with your partner to write a paragraph about pollution in
your partner's country. Use complete sentences. Use the present tense and the present continuous
tense when each is appropriate.

_____

_____

_____

_____

_____

_____

_____

K.   READING A CHART: *WITH YOUR CLASS*

Look at Chart 3.4 on the following page and then answer these questions.

1. How many people (what percent) are telling strangers to pick up their litter?
2. Are people cutting back on air conditioning and heating?
3. How many people (what percent) are using public transportation often?
4. Are most people using less water when they brush their teeth?
5. How many people (what percent) are recycling newspapers, bottles, or cans?

CHART 3.4

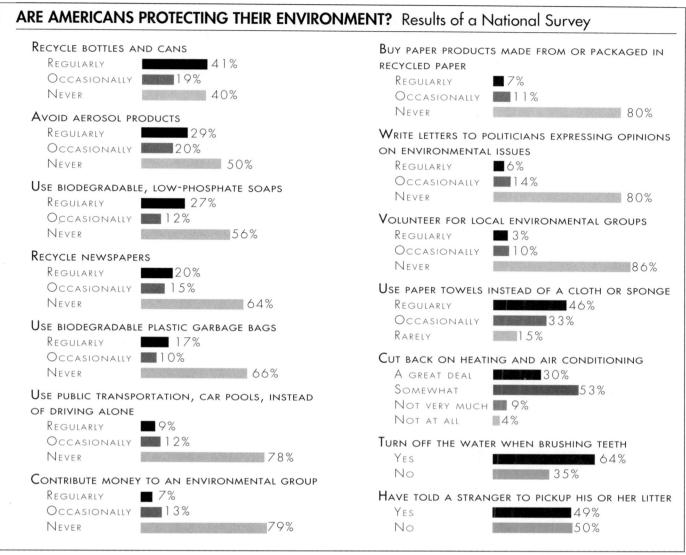

ARE AMERICANS PROTECTING THEIR ENVIRONMENT? Results of a National Survey

RECYCLE BOTTLES AND CANS
REGULARLY 41%
OCCASIONALLY 19%
NEVER 40%

AVOID AEROSOL PRODUCTS
REGULARLY 29%
OCCASIONALLY 20%
NEVER 50%

USE BIODEGRADABLE, LOW-PHOSPHATE SOAPS
REGULARLY 27%
OCCASIONALLY 12%
NEVER 56%

RECYCLE NEWSPAPERS
REGULARLY 20%
OCCASIONALLY 15%
NEVER 64%

USE BIODEGRADABLE PLASTIC GARBAGE BAGS
REGULARLY 17%
OCCASIONALLY 10%
NEVER 66%

USE PUBLIC TRANSPORTATION, CAR POOLS, INSTEAD OF DRIVING ALONE
REGULARLY 9%
OCCASIONALLY 12%
NEVER 78%

CONTRIBUTE MONEY TO AN ENVIRONMENTAL GROUP
REGULARLY 7%
OCCASIONALLY 13%
NEVER 79%

BUY PAPER PRODUCTS MADE FROM OR PACKAGED IN RECYCLED PAPER
REGULARLY 7%
OCCASIONALLY 11%
NEVER 80%

WRITE LETTERS TO POLITICIANS EXPRESSING OPINIONS ON ENVIRONMENTAL ISSUES
REGULARLY 6%
OCCASIONALLY 14%
NEVER 80%

VOLUNTEER FOR LOCAL ENVIRONMENTAL GROUPS
REGULARLY 3%
OCCASIONALLY 10%
NEVER 86%

USE PAPER TOWELS INSTEAD OF A CLOTH OR SPONGE
REGULARLY 46%
OCCASIONALLY 33%
RARELY 15%

CUT BACK ON HEATING AND AIR CONDITIONING
A GREAT DEAL 30%
SOMEWHAT 53%
NOT VERY MUCH 9%
NOT AT ALL 4%

TURN OFF THE WATER WHEN BRUSHING TEETH
YES 64%
NO 35%

HAVE TOLD A STRANGER TO PICKUP HIS OR HER LITTER
YES 49%
NO 50%

SOURCE: USA TODAY. INFORMATION REPRINTED WITH PERMISSION

L. TAKING A SURVEY: *IN PAIRS*

What are students on your campus doing to help clean up the environment? Find out by taking a survey. Use the information in the chart above to help you think of at least five more questions like the ones below. Then, survey ten students around campus and report the results in class. Report your findings in percentages. Do the results match those in the chart above?

1. Are you using less water?
2. Are you recycling cans, bottles, and papers?
3. Are you driving less?

4. _____

5. _____

6. _____

7. _____

8. _____

FIGURE 4.1 Types of Farming Around the World

Agriculture
CHAPTER 4

Types of Farming
LESSON 1

A. WARM-UP: *IN SMALL GROUPS*

Discuss these questions with your classmates: What do you know about farmers in your country? Is anyone in your family a farmer? Were your grandparents or great-grandparents farmers? What can you tell the group about farmers in your country? Use the questions below to help you continue with your discussion.

1. Where do farmers in your country live? In what part of your country?
2. Is farming a good business? Can farmers make a lot of money?
3. Do most farmers have large farms?
4. Do farmers work all year?
5. What crops do farmers grow?
6. What kinds of animals do they raise?
7. Do young people in your country want to become farmers?

B. SUMMARIZE AND COMPARE

B.1. Making a List: *In Small Groups and With Your Class*

With your group, make a chart listing the kinds of farms in the different parts of the world represented by the students in your group. Next, each group should share its list with the entire class. Are the lists different? Why do you think that they are different?

CHART 4.1

Country	Types of Farming

B.2. Written Practice: *On Your Own*

Use the information on your chart and from the class discussion to write sentences comparing types of farming in different parts of the world. Follow the model.

MODEL: *Farmers in Japan produce less beef than farmers in Argentina produce.*

1. _____

2. _____

3. _____

4. _____

5. _____

C. FOCUS VOCABULARY: *ON YOUR OWN*

On the lines below, write down new words that you learn in class. Add to your list as you study types of farming. Focus on new verbs and nouns.

_____	_____	_____
_____	_____	_____
_____	_____	_____
_____	_____	_____
_____	_____	_____

D. READING

Farming

Importance of Farming

Farmers are important to everyone because they grow the food that people need. Farmers are an important part of the economy of every country. In some countries, agriculture is the main industry. In nearly every country, the government tries to help farmers because their work is so vital. In the United States, there are three main types of farms: general, specialized, and corporate.

General Farming

General farmers grow crops and raise animals. They usually live on the farm and keep some of the food that they produce for their families to use, selling the rest. The types of crops that they can raise depends on the climate of their area. In the past, most farmers were general farmers, growing several different crops and raising a few animals, too.

Specialized Farming

These days, farmers in the United States and in many other countries are planting only one or two kinds of crops, or they are raising only one or two types of animals. For example, these specialized farmers grow only wheat or only soybeans. They usually sell all of their crop to a food company which processes the food and prepares it for the supermarket.

Other specialized farmers raise only one or two types of animals. For example, a dairy farmer raises cows only for milk. A poultry farmer raises only chickens, turkeys, or ducks for meat and eggs.

Corporate Farming

Often, a food-processing company will buy farm land and raise the food that it needs for its business. For example, a large soup company might raise tomatoes, mushrooms, and beans so that it will be sure of having the ingredients that it needs to make its soups. In addition, owning farmland can help to control the cost of making the soups. This is known as corporate farming.

Corporate, specialized, and general farming are all important to the country's economy.

E. TRUE OR FALSE: *ON YOUR OWN*

Look at each statement below about the reading and circle *True* or *False*. If the statement is false, correct it.

1. Specialized farmers grow many types of crops.   **True**   **False**

_____

2. There are two main types of farms in the United States.   **True**   **False**

_____

3. In the past, most farmers were specialized.   **True**   **False**

_____

4. The governments of almost all countries try to support farmers.   **True**   **False**

_____

5. Dairy farmers raise cows and sell their meat.   **True**   **False**

_____

6. Food companies usually buy a general farmer's entire crop.   **True**   **False**

_____

7. Specialized farmers usually sell their crops to food-processing companies.   **True**   **False**

_____

8. Corporate farms are not usually large.   **True**   **False**

_____

9. Modern United States farmers are usually specialized.   **True**   **False**

_____

10. A poultry farmer produces meat and eggs.   **True**   **False**

_____

F. TAKING NOTES: *On Your Own*

Use the information from the reading to complete the chart below. List facts that are true for each type of farm and facts that are true for all three types of farm.

CHART 4.2

General Farm	Specialized Farm	Corporate Farm	All Three

G. READING A MAP: *In Small Groups and On Your Own*

G.1. Oral Practice: *In Small Groups*

Look at the map at right of the United States and Canada. Work together to answer the questions below. Discuss your answers in class.

1. In what parts of the United States do farmers produce the most corn?
2. Where is sugar cane growing, according to this map?
3. Where are farmers growing cotton?
4. Where are most of the manufacturing centers located?
5. What are the principal crops of Hawaii?
6. Is rice grown in the United States?

G.2. Written Practice: *On Your Own*

Write a short paragraph about agricultural production in your country. What crops grow there? In what parts of the country do they grow? Are there any common crops that do not grow in your country? (If you do not know about your country, write about the United States, using the information from the map in Figure 4.2.)

_____

_____

_____

_____

_____

_____

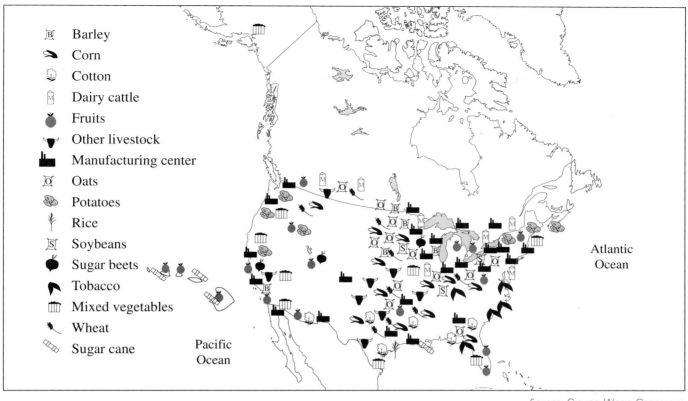

Barley
Corn
Cotton
Dairy cattle
Fruits
Other livestock
Manufacturing center
Oats
Potatoes
Rice
Soybeans
Sugar beets
Tobacco
Mixed vegetables
Wheat
Sugar cane

Pacific
Ocean

Atlantic
Ocean

SOURCE: GLENCO WORLD GEOGRAPHY

FIGURE 4.2

TABLE 4.1   Study the patterns for talking about **continuous actions vs. habits and facts**.

Farmers	always usually	**plant**	seed	early	in the spring.
		are planting			this spring.

H.   WRITTEN PRACTICE: *ON YOUR OWN*

Complete each sentence with the present or present continuous form of the verb in parentheses. Follow the models and the patterns in Table 4.1.

MODEL   (cut down) A farmer usually ___*cuts down*___ plants in the fall.

(rain / negative) This summer it ___*isn't raining*___ very much.

1. (be) Most farmers _____ busy every month of the year.

2. (break up) In the spring, farmers _____ the land with a plow.

3. (plant) This spring, farmers _____ more wheat than they did last year.

4. (make) The warm sun _____ the seeds grow.

5. (use) This year, farmers _____ less insecticide than they did in the past.

6. (harvest / negative) A farmer _____ the crops before they are ripe.

7. (plant / negative) Last year the farmer planted corn, but this year he _____ it.

8. (work) Farmers always _____ very hard.

9. (help) Where are the farmer's children now? They _____ their parents with the animals.

10. (sell) Farmers _____ crops in the city.

11. (produce / negative) Farmers in the northern part of the United States _____ cotton.

12. (grow) These days farmers _____ less wheat and more corn.

I. LISTENING PRACTICE: *ON YOUR OWN*

Listen to what your teacher tells you about farming during the year. As you listen, fill in the chart below with information about farm activities in different seasons.

CHART 4.3

Spring	Summer	Autumn / Fall	Winter

J. USING YOUR NOTES

In class, take turns telling your teacher what information you have on your chart. Then, use the information on your chart to write about what the farmer does in each season.

In the spring _____

_____

_____

_____

_____

_____

In the summer _____

_____

_____

_____

_____

_____

In the autumn _____

_____

_____

_____

_____

In the winter _____

_____

_____

_____

_____

_____

K.   ORAL PRACTICE: *WITH YOUR CLASS*

Use the cues below to make sentences using *before* or *after*. Use the simple present tense. Use *the farmer* or *the farmers* as the subject of one clause of the sentences. Follow the model.

MODEL: prepare the soil / plant seeds   (before)
                    The farmer prepares the soil before she plants the seeds.

1. harvest the crop / plans for the next year   (after)
2. harvest the crops / sell the crops   (before)
3. calculate the profits / sell the cattle   (after)
4. plant the seeds / decide how much seed to buy   (before)
5. must finish his work / have time to go fishing   (before)
6. repair the farm equipment / prepare the field   (after)
7. raise the crops / harvest the crops   (after)
8. sell the crops / buy new equipment   (before)

L. ORAL PRACTICE: *IN PAIRS*

With your partner, ask questions about what is happening in each picture. Take turns answering each other's questions.

FIGURE 4.3

MODELS:

Ask about the person.
  Partner A: *Who is feeding the animals?*
  Partner B: *The woman is feeding them.*

Ask about the animals.
  Partner A: *What is the animal doing?*
  Partner B: *It is eating.*

FIGURE 4.4

1. Ask about the machine.

2. Ask about the place

3. Ask about the activity

4. Ask about the time.

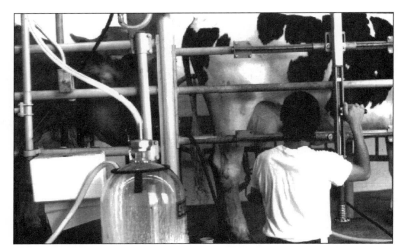

FIGURE 4.5

5. Ask about the activity.

6. Ask about the animals

7. Ask about the machine.

8. Ask about the place.

(Top) Spencer Grant © Stock Boston, Inc.; (middle) Robert Houser © 1991 COMSTOCK; (bottom) M. Antman © The Image Works

The Business of Farming
LESSON 2

CHART 4.4

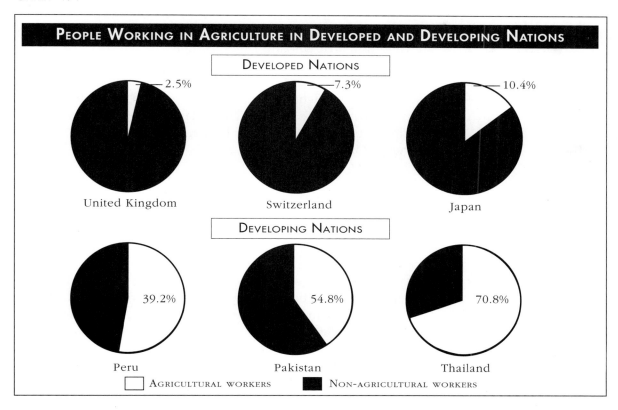

PEOPLE WORKING IN AGRICULTURE IN DEVELOPED AND DEVELOPING NATIONS

DEVELOPED NATIONS

2.5% — United Kingdom
7.3% — Switzerland
10.4% — Japan

DEVELOPING NATIONS

39.2% — Peru
54.8% — Pakistan
70.8% — Thailand

□ AGRICULTURAL WORKERS   ■ NON-AGRICULTURAL WORKERS

A.   WARM-UP: *WITH YOUR CLASS*

Look at the charts above. What do they tell you about the business of farming in some parts of the world? Are you surprised by the percentage of farmers in the countries represented? Do you think that the number of farmers in the world is increasing or decreasing? Why? Discuss your ideas with your class.

B.   FOCUS VOCABULARY: *ON YOUR OWN*

On the lines below, write down new words that you learn in class. Add to your list as you study about the business of farming. Focus on new nouns, verbs, and adjectives.

_____   _____   _____

_____   _____   _____

_____   _____   _____

_____   _____   _____

_____   _____   _____

C. READING

Farming

What a Farmer Must Know

Farming is a difficult business. Farmers must know what crops will be the most profitable, when to plant, how much seed to buy, and what kinds of fertilizer and pesticides to use. In addition, they must understand the weather conditions in their area and how that will affect their business.

Some farmers do not grow crops; they raise animals. In this case, the farmers must know what to feed the animals, how to take care of them when they are sick or injured, when to breed them and when to sell them. These days, farmers often study veterinary medicine and animal husbandry to make their business more successful.

Selling the Crops

Because modern farmers produce large amounts of crops and large numbers of animals to sell, they don't usually try to sell their produce and animals directly to the people who are going to eat it. Instead, they generally sell them to large food companies, which often make contracts with the farmers to buy their products. Because of this, specialized farming is becoming more and more important.

Specialized farmers sell everything they raise to one company. This can be good for the farmers since they know that there will be someone to buy their crop. Selling food to a big company also protects the farmers from low prices. At the same time, specialized farming can also be dangerous for the farmers' business. If the weather is bad during the growing season or if insects damage the crops, the farmers will lose a lot of money. Moreover, if the price of the product goes up after the farmers have signed a contract with a food-processing company or a supermarket, they may lose money because they agreed to sell at a lower price.

General farmers often raise several different crops which have different growing seasons and harvesting schedules. In this way, general farmers may be more protected than are specialized farmers. If general farmers lose one or two crops during the year, they will still have other crops to sell. General farmers often sell directly to consumers. Because of this, the number of buyers is not certain, and this can cause the price of the crops to go up or down during the year. In most cases, general farmers don't make as much money as do specialized farmers.

D. OUTLINING: *ON YOUR OWN*

Use the information in the reading above to complete the following outline.

I. Farmers must know many things about crops.

A. _____

B. _____

C. They must know how much seed to buy.

D. _____

E. _____

II. Farmers must know many things about animals.

A. _____

B. _____

C. _____

D. They must know when to sell them.

III. Modern farmers produce large amounts of crops and large numbers of animals.

A. They don't sell the crops and animals to consumers.

B. _____

IV. Specialized farmers sell all of their crops to one company.

A. There are two advantages to this.

1. _____

2. _____

B. _____

1. _____

2. Prices may go up after the farmer signs the contract.

V. General farmers raise many types of crops throughout the year.

A. _____

1. They don't depend on only one crop.

B. _____

1. They don't make much money.

E.   DISCUSSION: *WITH YOUR CLASS*

Talk about these questions with your class and teacher.

1. Bad weather and insects can destroy crops and make the farmer lose money. What else can you think of that might damage crops?
2. Are insecticides good? Why or why not? Are there other ways that farmers can control damage from insects?
3. What about fertilizers? Are they good or bad?
4. Are there crops that grow in only one region of your country?
5. Can farmers grow crops all year round in your country?

TABLE 4.2   Study the patterns for using **have to** and **must**.

A farmer	**must** **has to**	work all year long.
Most farmers	**must** **have to**	make money at harvest time.

Study the difference in meaning between must not and don't have to.

A farmer Farmers	**doesn't have to** **don't have to**	grow the same crop in every field. take vacations every year.
	BUT	
Farmers A farmer	**must not** **must not**	use too much insecticide on their crops. let his fields get very dry.

FIGURE 4.6

F.   ORAL AND WRITTEN PRACTICE: *WITH YOUR CLASS*

Talk about the pictures above with your class. Then, following the patterns in Table 4.2, write four sentences about each subject listed below. Use *have to* or *must* in your sentences. Try to use *don't / doesn't have to* or *must not* in a few of your sentences. The first sentence is done for you.

Weather

1. *The farmer must wait for warm weather before he can plant.*

2. _____

3. _____

4. _____

Crops

1. _____

2. _____

3. _____

4. _____

Animals

1. _____

2. _____

3. _____

4. _____

TABLE 4.3   Study the patterns for using **frequency words.**

Farmers	**always** **usually** **often** **sometimes** **seldom** **rarely** **never**	take their crops to market in the fall.

G.   WRITTEN PRACTICE: *ON YOUR OWN*

G.1. Using Frequency Words

Answer these questions using *always, usually, often, sometimes, seldom, rarely,* or *never* in your answers. Follow the model and the patterns in Table 4.3.

<u>MODEL:</u>   How often does a farmer plant seeds in the winter?

_____ A farmer never plants seeds in the winter. _____

1. How often does a farmer need to get a good price for his crop?

_____

2. How often do a farmer's animals get sick?

_____

3. How often does it rain in the summer in your area?

_____

4. How often do farmers raise food only for their own families?

_____

5. How often does a general farmer sell his crops to a food-processing company?

_____

TABLE 4.4   Study the patterns for talking about time with **when**, **while**, and **every time**.

Farmers must sell their crops	**when** **while** **every time**	prices are high.

G.2. Talking about Time

Now answer these questions, using *when*, *while*, or *every time* in your answer. Follow the model and the patterns in Table 4.4.

MODEL: When do farmers need to irrigate their crops?

They need to irrigate them when the weather is dry.

1. When does a farmer need to know about medicine?

_____

2. When does a farmer have to worry about the weather?

_____

3. When does a farmer have to buy seed?

_____

4. When does a farmer sell his crops to a food-processing company?

_____

5. When does a farmer try to get a good price for his crops?

_____

The Changing American Farmer

A. WARM-UP: *WITH YOUR CLASS*

Look at Chart 4.5 and then discuss these questions with your classmates.

1. What is happening to the number of farmers in the United States?
2. What about the number of acres that are farmed?
3. In 1910, it took more than 13 million farmers to feed the population (approximately 90 million people). Today there are fewer than 4 million farmers in the United States, but the population is more than 239 million. How is it possible for fewer farmers to feed more people?
4. What role has technology played in food production?

CHART 4.5

Farm Employment and Production, 1910 through 1984			
YEAR	ACRES FARMED	FARMERS	TOTAL POPULATION
1910	879,000,000	13,555,000	92,400,000
1930	987,000,000	12,497,000	123,200,000
1950	1,202,000,000	9,926,000	151,7000,000
1970	1,102,000,000	4,523,000	205,100,000
1985	1,014,000,000	3,470,000	239,300,000

B. FOCUS VOCABULARY: *ON YOUR OWN*

On the lines below, write down new words that you learn in class. Add to your list as you study the changing American farmer. Focus on new adverbs and adjectives.

_____   _____   _____

_____   _____   _____

_____   _____   _____

_____   _____   _____

_____   _____   _____

_____   _____   _____

C. LISTENING PRACTICE: *ON YOUR OWN*

Listen to the information that your teacher gives you about how farming in the United States is changing. Fill in the chart below as you listen.

CHART 4.6

Farm Family	Corporate Farming	New Methods of Farming

D. WRITTEN PRACTICE

Use the information from the chart you made above to answer questions about how farming is changing. Follow the model.

MODEL: How is the size of the farm family changing?

The farm family is getting smaller.

1. Why are there fewer family farms today? Give two reasons.

_____

_____

2. What are farmers using now to do the farm work?

_____

_____

3. What are farm families buying in the city?

_____

_____

4. Why do many large food companies have their own farms?

_____

_____

5. What new method is going to help farmers grow more food?

_____

_____

6. How are farmers changing the way they raise animals? Give two ways.

_____

_____

7. How are scientists helping farmers? Mention two ways.

_____

_____

E. PROBLEM SOLVING: *IN SMALL GROUPS*

Work in small groups to solve this problem. Read the description of the problem and the two possible solutions. After you have read each solution, make a list of its advantages and disadvantages. Then, compare your solutions with those of the other groups, and discuss them with each other. Do you have other ideas about how Mr. Jones can use his land?

Mr. Jones owns 100 acres of land in the central part of the United States. He has two part-time workers and two teenaged children who can help him after school and on weekends. The Jones farm is small, and Mr. Jones must decide how to use his land to get the biggest profits. Here are two possible solutions. What should he do?

Solution 1
He can use all of his land to plant corn. He can plant it in the spring and harvest it in the late summer. He could sell it to a large food-processing company for a fair price.

CHART 4.7

Advantages	Disadvantages

Solution 2

He can use his land to plant ten different types of crops. The broccoli and strawberries would be ready to harvest in the early summer. Tomatoes and corn would be ready in late summer. Potatoes and apples would be ready in the fall. He could use some of the land to raise rabbits and honeybees.

CHART 4.8

Advantages	Disadvantages

F. WRITTEN PRACTICE: *ON YOUR OWN*

How is agriculture changing around the world? Take some time to think of some questions about the family farm, corporate farming, and new methods of farming. Write your questions below.

1. _____

2. _____

3. _____

4. _____

5. _____

G. INTERVIEW: *IN PAIRS*

Now work with a partner. Ask him or her the questions that you wrote in the previous exercise. Also ask your partner about agriculture in his or her country. Record the answers in the chart below.

CHART 4.9

Farm Family	Corporate Farming	New Methods of Farming

H. WRITTEN PRACTICE: *ON YOUR OWN*

Use the information in the chart above to write a paragraph about how farming is changing in your partner's country. The first sentence has been started for you.

Farming is changing in _____

_____

_____

_____

_____

_____

_____

_____

_____

_____

Figure 5.1   A Small Town in the 1850s

A Small Town in the 1850s

CHAPTER 5

Home Life in a Small Town

LESSON 1

A. **WARM-UP:** *IN SMALL GROUPS*

Look at the picture about life in an American small town in the past. Can you describe what is different in these pictures from the way that people in the United States live today? When you are ready, compare your descriptions with those of the other groups in your class. Ask your teacher to check your vocabulary.

B. **FOCUS VOCABULARY:** *ON YOUR OWN*

On the lines below, write down any new words that you learn in class. Add to your list as you study about American life in the past. Focus on nouns and verbs.

_____   _____   _____

_____   _____   _____

_____   _____   _____

_____   _____   _____

_____   _____   _____

C. **READING**   *Population Shift*

Today in the United States more people live in large cities than in small towns. In the past, however, the opposite was true. In the nineteenth century, ninety percent of the population lived on farms or in small towns. The United States was mainly an agricultural country then. Both the farmers and the people in the small towns depended on each other. The farmers came into the town to sell their crops; to buy goods that they could not make for themselves; or to use the professional services of a doctor, a lawyer, and so forth. The merchants and the professional people needed to live in the small towns so that they could be close to the farmers. In 1910, two out of three Americans still lived in small towns and rural areas, but thirty years later, in 1940, two out of three Americans lived in cities. Today more than ninety percent of Americans live in urban areas.

D. DISCUSSION: *WITH YOUR CLASS*

Now discuss these questions with your classmates.

1. Where do most people in your country live? On farms, in small towns, or in cities?
2. Where did most people in your country live in the past?
3. Why did the population move?
4. What do you think is different about life in a small town and life in a city?

TABLE 5.1   **Study the patterns for asking and answering questions with was and were.**

be			The road	**was**	unpaved.	
	Was		the road		unpaved ?	
						Yes, it **was** unpaved. Yes, it **was**.
be			The houses	**were**	made of wood.	
	Were		the houses		made of wood?	
						Yes, they **were** made of wood. **Were** the houses made of steel? No, they **weren't** made of steel. No, they **weren't**.

E. ORAL PRACTICE: *IN PAIRS*

E.1. Asking and Answering Questions

Ask and answer questions with your partner, using the cue words below. Follow the patterns in Table 5.1. Practice both the long and short forms in your answers.

MODELS: the road / be / unpaved
        Partner A: *Was the road unpaved?*
        Partner B: *Yes. It was unpaved.*
            OR
        Yes, it was.

      there / be / buildings / in the town
        Partner A: *Were there tall buildings in the town?*
        Partner B: *No, there weren't tall buildings.*
            OR
        No, there weren't.

1. the houses / be / made of wood
2. the town / be / small
3. the road / be / paved
4. the post office / be / in the general store
5. there / be / many small shops
6. there / be / many kinds of medicine in the pharmacy
7. women's dresses / be / short
8. the shops / be / in the center of the town

TABLE 5.2   Study the patterns for asking and answering questions about **actions in the past**.

visit		The doctor	**visited**	sick people at home.
	Did	the doctor	**visit**	sick people at home?
stay		Travelers	**stayed**	at the inn.
	Did	travelers	**stay**	at the inn?
study		Children	**studied**	in a one-room school house.
	Did	children	**study**	in a one-room school house?
chop		People	**chopped**	wood for the fireplace.
	Did	people	**chop**	wood for the fireplace?

SPELLING RULES:

Consonant + **-y**	becomes **-ied**	**studied**
Vowel + -y	only adds -ed	stayed
Vowel + Consonant	doubles the consonant	chopped

E.2. Asking and Answering Questions

Ask and answer questions with your partner, using the cue words below. Follow the patterns in Table 5.2. Use both long and short forms in your answers.

MODEL: animals / walk / in the road
            Partner A: *Did animals walk in the road?*
            Partner B: *Yes. They walked in the road.*
                OR
                Yes, they did.

1. horses / pull / the wagons
2. women / cook / in the fireplace
3. the doctor / visit / sick people
4. the printer / publish / the newspaper
5. people / live / in small houses

6. people / mail / letters / in the general store
7. people / burn / candles / at night
8. men / chop / wood / for the fireplace
9. women / sew / clothes / at home
10. travelers / stay / at the inn

TABLE 5.3   Study the patterns for some **irregular verbs in the past**.

teach		One teacher	**taught**	all the children.
	Did	one teacher	**teach**	all the children?
wear		Women	**wore**	long dresses.
	Did	women	**wear**	long dresses?

Irregular Verbs			
build	**built**	grow	**grew**
buy	**bought**	make	**made**
drink	**drank**	sell	**sold**
get	**got**	sleep	**slept**
go	**went**		

E.3. Asking and Answering Questions

Ask and answer questions with your partner, using the cue words below. Follow the patterns in Table 5.3. Use both long and short forms in your answers.

MODEL: people / buy / stamps / in the general store
        Partner A: *Did people buy stamps in the general store?*
        Partner B: *Yes. They bought stamps in the general store.*
                 OR
        Yes, they did.

1. women / wear / long dresses
2. people / drink / tea from herbs
3. the gunsmith / make / rifles
4. travelers / sleep / at the inn
5. people / get / water / from a well
6. one teacher / teach / all the children
7. the general store / sell / many kinds of merchandise
8. people / build / their houses / with wood
9. women / grow / vegetables / in the garden
10. people / go / to church / on Sunday

F. READING   *Family Life in a Small Town*

Houses

Families in small towns lived in houses near the center of the town. They built their houses with wood or sometimes bricks. The houses were usually not big and had only one story. People often put up a fence around the house to keep the animals away. Near the house there was a small garden where the housewife grew vegetables and herbs. The family used the vegetables for cooking, and they made tea and medicine from the herbs. Behind the house, the animals stayed in a barn. Almost every family had a horse and chickens, and maybe some pigs and a cow.

FIGURE 5.2

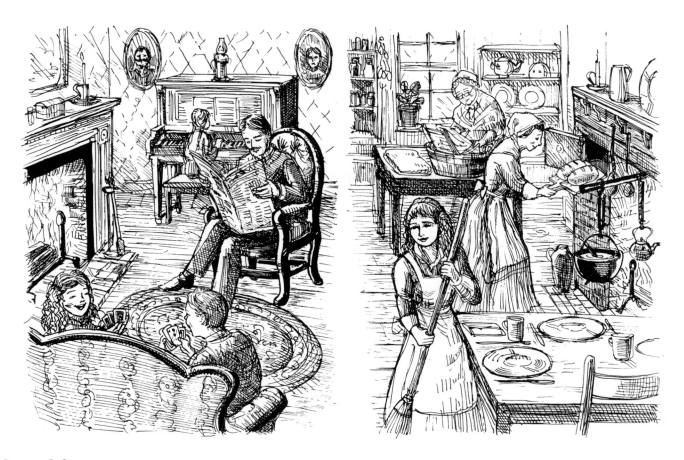

FIGURE 5.3

Inside the House: The Parlor

Inside the house, the main rooms were the kitchen and the parlor. The parlor was a special room in the house. When guests visited the family, they sat and talked in the parlor. Here the family kept their best furniture. There usually was a cabinet for their good dishes, a sofa, some comfortable chairs, and a rug. Music was important to them. Because they did not have radios or stereos, the family often had a piano in the parlor, which they liked to play at night. While someone played the piano, the other members of the family listened or sang songs. There was no electricity, so people burned candles or oil lamps for light.

The Kitchen

The kitchen was the other main room in the house. The family actually spent most of its time in this room. There was always a fireplace in the kitchen. The men chopped wood outside and brought it inside to the kitchen. They made a fire in the fireplace, and the women cooked the food there. The fireplace also provided heat for the house. Women worked all day in the kitchen. In addition to preparing and cooking food, they washed and ironed clothes, sewed new clothes, and made things such as candles and soap. They dried the herbs from the garden and hung them on the wall. They used the herbs all year long for cooking, making tea, and making medicine. The kitchen was a busy place. The family ate their meals there, and in the evening, after working all day, they often sat near the fireplace and relaxed. They read the newspaper and talked about the town news. Sometimes they played cards or games like checkers and chess.

Housekeeping

Housekeeping was not easy. People had to clean the fireplace and make a new fire every day. Houses did not have plumbing. When they needed water, they went outside and got water from the well. They carried the water in a bucket into the kitchen where they used it for cooking, washing, and drinking. Women swept the floor with a broom because they didn't have vacuum cleaners. They washed the clothes and dishes in a tub because they didn't have washing machines and dishwashers. People did not buy as many things in the stores as we do today. They tried to make things at home. Women baked bread for the family at home, preserved food in jars for the winter, mended old clothes, and made new clothes for the family. Men took care of the horses and other animals, cut down trees and chopped wood for the fireplace, and made furniture for the family. The whole family got up early every day and worked hard. At night they went to bed early because they did not want to use up their candles quickly. The family had a lot of work to do in the 1850s. They didn't have modern conveniences, but they thought that their life was more comfortable than life was before them!

TABLE 5.4   Study the patterns for **new irregular verbs** from the reading above.

bring	**brought**	read	**read**
cut	**cut**	sit	**sat**
eat	**ate**	spend	**spent**
hang	**hung**	sweep	**swept**
have	**had**	take	**took**
keep	**kept**	think	**thought**
put	**put**		

G.   COMPREHENSION: *ON YOUR OWN*

G.1. True or False

Read each statement about the reading and then circle *True* or *False*. If the statement is false, correct it.

1. People bought new clothes often.   **True**   **False**

   _____

2. The family spent most of their time in the parlor.   **True**   **False**

   _____

3. Fences kept the animals away from the houses.   **True**   **False**

   _____

4. People made many things they needed at home.   **True**   **False**

   _____

5. Guests talked to the family in the kitchen.   **True**   **False**

   _____

6. The piano was an important form of entertainment.   **True**   **False**

_____

7. Herbs were useful for making tea and medicine.   **True**   **False**

_____

8. Drinking water came from the well outside.   **True**   **False**

_____

9. People didn't have time to relax.   **True**   **False**

_____

10. The family put their best furniture in the parlor.   **True**   **False**

_____

G.2. Comprehension Questions

Answer the following questions about the reading. Write a complete sentence to answer each question. Follow the patterns in Table 5.4.

1. When did the family use the parlor?

_____

2. What did the family do in the evening to relax?

_____

3. How did the family save money?

_____

4. Why was housekeeping difficult?

_____

5. Why did the family spend a lot of time in the kitchen?

_____

H.   DISCUSSION: *WITH YOUR CLASS*

1. How is family life different now from the way it was in the past?
2. Where does the family spend most of their time today?
3. Do you think families had more or less time to be together in the past? Why?
4. How was family life in the past different from family life today in your country?

TABLE 5.5   Study the patterns for making **negative statements in the past.**

Regular Verb live	People They	**lived** **didn't live**	in small houses. in big houses.
Irregular Verb drink	People They	**drank** **didn't drink**	tea from herbs. much coffee.

I.   WRITTEN PRACTICE: *ON YOUR OWN*

Use the verbs below to fill in the blanks in the sentences. All of the sentences are about life in the past. Follow the models and the patterns in Tables 5.4 and 5.5.

MODELS: heat

People in the past ___*didn't heat*___ their houses with a furnace.

They ___*heated*___ their houses with a fireplace.

sit

People in the past ___*didn't sit*___ in the parlor often.

They ___*sat*___ in the parlor when they had guests.

1. (wash) People in the past _____ their clothes in a washing machine.

   They _____ their clothes in a big tub.

2. (cook) People in the past _____ on a stove.

   They _____ in a fireplace.

3. (have) People in the past _____ electric lights.

   They _____ candles and oil lamps.

4. (go) People in the past _____ to bed late at night.

   They _____ to bed early.

5. (eat) People in the past _____ in a dining room.

   They _____ their meals in the kitchen.

6. (sew) People in the past _____ their clothes on a sewing machine.

   They _____ their clothes by hand with a needle and thread.

7. (listen) People in the past _____ to music on the radio.

   They _____ to piano music in the parlor.

8. (get) People in the past _____ water from the sink.

   They _____ water from the well outside.

9. (live) People in the past _____ in a suburb.

   They _____ close to the center of the town.

10. (think) People in the past _____ their life was hard.

   They _____ their life was comfortable.

J.   ORAL PRACTICE: *IN PAIRS*

Follow the models to ask and answer questions about life in the past. First, Partner A uses the cue words below to ask a question. Then, Partner B answers the question and says another sentence to explain the answer. Use the information in the reading on pages 114–116. When you are finished, check your answers with your classmates' answers.

MODELS: people in the past / work / hard
     Partner A: *Did people in the past work hard?*
     Partner B: *Yes, they did.*
     (New sentence) *They worked hard all day.*

    women in the past / buy / bread / in a store
     Partner A: *Did women in the past buy bread in a store?*
     Partner B: *No, they didn't.*
     (New Sentence) *They baked bread at home.*

1. people in the past / live / in small houses
2. families in the past / spend / a lot of time / in the kitchen
3. houses in the past / have / plumbing
4. men in the past / take care / of the animals / in the barn
5. people in the past / stay up / late at night
6. women in the past / buy / clothes / in a store
7. men in the past / cut down / trees / for firewood
8. people in the past / use / electric lights
9. families in the past / keep / animals / in the house
10. houses in the past / have / many rooms

K.   WRITTEN PRACTICE: *ON YOUR OWN*

Now, using the lines below, write the questions and answers for Exercise J. You can use the same answers that you gave with your partner and with your classmates, or you can change the answers.

_____

_____

_____

_____

_____

_____

_____

_____

_____

_____

_____

_____

_____

_____

L. ORAL PRACTICE: *WITH YOUR CLASS*

With your classmates, think about the differences between family life in the past and family life today. Take turns writing important words and ideas on the chalkboard. Use the lines below to write notes from the discussion. Try to find five or more differences for each topic listed.

Topic: The Parlor

_____

_____

_____

_____

Topic: The Kitchen

_____

_____

_____

_____

Topic: Housekeeping

_____

_____

_____

_____

Topic: Relaxation and Entertainment

_____

_____

_____

Topic: Conveniences

_____

_____

_____

_____

_____

_____

_____

_____

M.   WRITTEN PRACTICE: _ON YOUR OWN_

Choose three of the topics from Exercise L.   Use your notes from the class discussion to write a paragraph about how family life in the past was different from family life today.   Write five or more sentences for each paragraph.

Topic: _____

_____

_____

_____

_____

_____

Topic: _____

_____

_____

_____

_____

_____

Topic: _____

_____

_____

_____

_____

_____

Public Life in a Small Town
LESSON 2

FIGURE 5.4

A. WARM-UP: *WITH YOUR CLASS*

Look at the pictures above, that show public life in a small town in the past. Try to describe what you see in each picture. What does it show that is different from what people do today?

B. FOCUS VOCABULARY: *ON YOUR OWN*

On the lines below, write down any new words that you learn in class. Add to your list as you study about public life in a small town in the past. Focus on nouns and verbs.

_____   _____   _____

_____   _____   _____

_____   _____   _____

_____   _____   _____

_____   _____   _____

C. READING   *Small-town Life*

Introduction: Public Life in a Small Town

The public and social life of a small town centered on the activities that brought people together on a daily or weekly basis. The general store and the town inn were places where the townspeople and farmers from the area often met their neighbors and could exchange news. Other commercial places where people had a chance to get together were the many small shops and offices that craftsmen and professional people had in the town. The blacksmith, the pharmacist, the printer, and the weaver were some of the commercial businesses that were important for the townspeople. A town also needed a doctor, a lawyer, a barber, a minister, a banker, and an undertaker. These people had offices in the center of the town. On Sunday, townspeople gathered in the church, and after the religious service there often was a social event that gave people time to spend with their neighbors.

The General Store

Every town had one store that sold many kinds of merchandise. This store was known as the general store. When families needed items that they couldn't make for themselves at home, they went to the general store. There they found dry goods such as flour, sugar, salt, spices, and other food items that they couldn't grow or make at home. The general store also sold hardware such as nails, hammers, and other tools, and materials such as needles, thread, and cloth for making clothes. The post office was in the general store. People bought stamps and sent letters from the general store. When mail arrived from another town, people picked it up at the general store. Because people often wanted to buy something in the general store and pick up their mail, the general store was a busy and popular place where people could talk and exchange news.

Craftsmen

Not everything that people needed was available in the general store. Craftsmen had small shops where they worked and made their products. There might be a shoemaker in the town who would make boots and shoes from leather. There might be a weaver who would weave cloth from wool and cotton to make clothes and blankets. There might be a potter who would make dishes and containers from clay or a cooper who would make buckets and barrels out of wood. There was always a blacksmith, who had a very important job in the town. The blacksmith made iron shoes for the horses and tools from iron for the farmers and townspeople. People often had to bring their horses to the blacksmith, so the blacksmith's shop was another social center for the town where people met each other. In some towns there was a printer. The printer published the local newspaper and printed advertisements. Then, if people didn't hear the news from their friends, they could read it in the newspaper.

Professional People

There were also professional people, who had offices in the center of the town. The townspeople needed a lawyer who understood the laws and could explain them. The doctor took care of sick people and cared for people who were injured in accidents. There was no hospital in the town. The doctor visited his patients in their homes and came every day until they recovered. Sometimes a town had a banker who lent people money when they didn't have enough. Sometimes there was a pharmacist who knew how to mix ingredients and prepare medicines. If there wasn't a pharmacist, the doctor would prepare the medicine for his patients. Barbers were men who did more than cut men's hair. There weren't many dentists, so the barber often tried to cure people's toothaches by pulling their teeth when they were bad. In a large town, the undertaker was also necessary. When a person died in the town, the undertaker dug the grave in the cemetery and buried the deceased.

The Inn

Traveling was difficult because roads were unpaved and conditions were bad. When people needed to travel to another town, they went in their wagon or they rode in a stagecoach. It took a long time to go even a short distance. The inn was the place where travelers stayed at night. The inn had a dining room on the ground floor where the travelers ate their meals and bedrooms on the second floor where they slept. Sometimes the inn didn't have enough beds for all the travelers and then strangers had to share beds! Since travelers from another town usually had interesting news to tell, the townspeople came to the inn at night to listen to the stories that the travelers told.

The Church

The town church was an important center for the townspeople. On Sunday, people put on their best clothes and assembled in the church for a religious service. The minister had an important role in the town's life. He conducted religious services on Sunday, performed marriage ceremonies, and conducted funerals. On Sunday, the people listened to the minister, who taught them about religion and led them in prayers. Singing was a main part of the religious service. People sang hymns and said prayers during the service. The activities in the church gave people an opportunity to meet friends who didn't come into town often during the week. When people got married, all the townspeople came and saw the ceremony. After the wedding, there was a party, where everyone ate good food, drank, laughed, and danced. Funerals were sad times, when people gathered because a person had died. Although it was a sad occasion, it was a part of the town's social life.

TABLE 5.6   Study the patterns for **new irregular verbs** from the reading above.

become	**became**	meet	**met**
can	**could**	ride	**rode**
come	**came**	see	**saw**
dig	**dug**	send	**sent**
feed	**fed**	sleep	**slept**
find	**found**	tell	**told**
give	**gave**	understand	**understood**
lead	**led**	weave	**wove**
lend	**lent**		

D.   COMPREHENSION: *ON YOUR OWN*

D.1. True or False

Read each statement about the reading and then circle *True* or *False*. If the statement is false, correct it.

1. The inn was a place where townspeople heard news.   **True**   **False**

_____

2. The general store sold everything that the townspeople needed.   **True**   **False**

_____

3. On Sunday, people were able to meet and talk to friends.   **True**   **False**

_____

4. The barber worked in the general store.   **True**   **False**

_____

5. When people were sick, they went to the hospital.   **True**   **False**

_____

6. The stagecoach delivered the mail to the town inn.   **True**   **False**

_____

7. Weddings and funerals were times for people to come together.   **True**   **False**

_____

8. The weaver wove cloth for making clothes.   **True**   **False**

_____

9. The potter was the town's shoemaker.   **True**   **False**

_____

10. The blacksmith made tools from iron.   **True**   **False**

D.2. Comprehension Questions

Answer the following questions about the reading. Write a complete sentence to answer each question. Follow the patterns in Table 5.6.

1. When did people in the past meet their friends and neighbors?

_____

2. How did people learn about the news from other towns?

_____

3. Why was traveling difficult?

_____

4. Why did people need to go to the general store often?

_____

5. What other craftsmen and professional people do you think the town probably had?

_____

TABLE 5.7   **Study the patterns for asking questions about life in the past.**

be	Where	**was**	the post office? The post office	**was**	in the general store.
	Where	**were**	the stores The stores	**were**	in the town? in the center of the town.
stay	Where	**did**	travelers Travelers	**stay** **stayed**	in the town ? at the inn.
buy	What	**did**	people People	**buy** **bought**	in the general store? dry goods in the general store.

E.   ORAL PRACTICE: *IN PAIRS*

Follow the patterns in Table 5.7 and the models below to ask questions about the past. Find the answer to each question in the list of activities. Use each activity only once.

make dishes and pots	weave cloth	cut hair and pull teeth
mix ingredients for medicine	explain the laws	make boots and shoes
fix tools and put on horseshoes	visit sick people	conduct religious services
dig graves and bury dead people	lend money	make buckets and barrels
publish the local newspaper	feed travelers and rent rooms	

MODELS: What / the potter / do
         Partner A: *What did the potter do?*
         Partner B: *The potter made dishes and pots.*

         What / the barber / do
         Partner A: *What did the barber do?*
         Partner B: *The barber cut hair and pulled teeth.*

1. What / the blacksmith / do
2. What / the doctor / do
3. What / the pharmacist / do
4. What / the weaver / do
5. What / the shoemaker / do
6. What / the lawyer / do
7. What / the undertaker / do
8. What / the innkeeper / do
9. What / the banker / do
10. What / the printer / do
11. What / the minister / do
12. What / the cooper / do

F. WRITTEN PRACTICE: *ON YOUR OWN*

Follow the models below to write questions and answers. Use the information in the reading to answer the questions. Check your answers with your classmates. Be sure to use correct punctuation.

MODELS: what / the blacksmith / fix

What did the blacksmith fix?

The blacksmith fixed iron tools.

where / travelers / sleep

Where did travelers sleep?

They slept at the inn.

1. where / people / buy / flour and sugar

_____

_____

2. what / the printer / publish

_____

_____

3. where / travelers / eat

_____

_____

4. what / the shoemaker / make / with leather

_____

_____

5. what / the cooper / have / in his shop

_____

_____

6. where / people / go / for weddings and funerals

_____

_____

7. where / the doctor / see / his patients

_____

_____

8. what / the lawyer / understand

_____

_____

9. where / the undertaker / dig / graves

_____

_____

10. what / people / wear / on Sundays

_____

_____

G. WRITTEN PRACTICE: *ON YOUR OWN*

Using the question word *what*, write questions about the underlined word or words in the following sentences. Follow the models and use correct punctuation.

MODELS: The pharmacist prepared <u>medicine</u> for the townspeople.

What did the pharmacist prepare for the townspeople?

Travelers told the townspeople <u>the news.</u>

What did travelers tell the townspeople?

1. The innkeeper rented the travelers <u>rooms</u>.

_____

2. The lawyer explained <u>the laws</u> to the townspeople.

_____

3. The owner of the general store sold the townspeople <u>dry goods and hardware</u>.

_____

4. The blacksmith repaired <u>tools</u> for the farmers.

_____

5. The stagecoach brought the townspeople <u>their mail</u>.

_____

6. The printer reported <u>the news</u> to the townspeople.

_____

7. The banker lent the townspeople <u>money</u>.

_____

8. The innkeeper cooked <u>meals</u> for the travelers.

_____

H.   ORAL PRACTICE: *IN PAIRS*

Using the question word *who*, take turns with your partner asking and answering questions. Follow the models.

MODELS: _____ / take care / of sick people / in their homes   (the doctor)
                Partner A: *Who took care of sick people in their homes?*
                Partner B: *The doctor did.*

        People / listen / to _____ / in the church / on Sunday   (the minister)
                Partner A: *Who did people listen to in the church on Sunday?*
                Partner B: *They listened to the minister in the church on Sunday.*

1. _____ / publish / the local newspaper   (the printer)
2. _____ / fix / tools / for the farmers   (the blacksmith)
3. People / talk / to _____ / about the laws   (the lawyer)
4. The innkeeper / rent / rooms / to _____   (travelers)
5. _____ / lend / the townspeople / money   (the banker)
6. _____ / operate / the post office   (the general storekeeper)
7. People / buy / dishes and pots / from _____   (the potter)
8. _____ / take care / of the cemetery   (the undertaker)

I.   WRITTEN PRACTICE: *ON YOUR OWN*

When you finish asking and answering the questions in Exercise H, write the questions and answers on the lines below.

_____

_____

_____

_____

TABLE 5.8   Study the patterns for talking about **habitual actions** in the past.

be	The post office	was	in the general store.
	The post office	**used to be**	in the general store.
	The stores	weren't	open on Sunday.
	The stores	**didn't use to be**	open on Sunday.
work	People in the past	worked	hard during the week.
	People in the past	**used to work**	hard during the week.
	They	didn't work	on Sunday.
	They	**didn't use to work**	on Sunday.

J.   WRITTEN PRACTICE: *ON YOUR OWN*

Using the cue words below, write sentences to talk about habits in the past. Follow the patterns in Table 5.8 and choose *used to* or *didn't use to* for each sentence. Then finish the sentence with an explanation. Use the information in the reading or your own ideas. Check your answers with your classmates' answers.

MODELS: People in the past / listen / to travelers / at the inn

People in the past used to listen to travelers at the inn

because   _they told stories about other towns._

People in the past / not receive / mail / every day

People in the past didn't use to receive mail every day

because   _the stagecoach didn't come to town every day._

1. Women / buy / cloth / from the weaver

_____

because _____

2. People / bring / horses / to the blacksmith

_____

because _____

3. The printer / collect / all the town news

_____

because _____

4. People in the past / not travel / often

_____

because _____

5. The barber / pull out / bad teeth

_____

because _____

6. People in the past / not stay up / late at night

_____

because _____

7. The owner of the general store / sell / stamps

_____

because _____

8. People in the past / wear / their best clothes / on Sunday

_____

because _____

K. WRITTEN PRACTICE: *ON YOUR OWN*

Using *used to* and *didn't use to* write sentences about what people did in the past and what people do today. Mention five habitual actions. Follow the models.

MODELS: *Today we buy our clothes in a store.*

In the past people didn't use to buy clothes in a store.

Women used to make clothes at home.

Today we get water inside the house.

In the past people didn't use to get water inside the house.

People used to go to the well for water.

1. _____

_____

_____

2. _____

_____

_____

3. _____

_____

_____

4. _____

_____

_____

5. _____

_____

_____

Education in the Past and Present
LESSON 3

FIGURE 5.5

A. WARM-UP: *WITH YOUR CLASS*

With your class, discuss the above pictures, which show what education was like in an American small town in the 1850s. Describe as many things as you can find in the pictures. Then answer these questions.

1. What things do you see in the pictures that you do not see in a modern school?
2. What are some things that a modern school has that you don't see in the pictures?
3. Do you think you would like to go to a school that was like the schools in the 1850s? Why or why not?

B. FOCUS VOCABULARY: *ON YOUR OWN*

On the lines below, write down any new words that you learn in class. Add to your list as you study about American education in the past. Focus on nouns and verbs.

_____   _____   _____

_____   _____   _____

_____   _____   _____

_____   _____   _____

_____   _____   _____

_____   _____   _____

C. LISTENING PRACTICE: *ON YOUR OWN*

Listen as your teacher describes what education was like for children in a small town in the 1850s. Your teacher will also explain some of the differences between schools in the past and schools today. Use the chart below for taking notes about the information.

CHART 5.1

	Schools in the 1850s	Modern Schools
Size		
Age of Children		
Travel to School		
Start of the School Day		
Desks		
Writing Materials		
Schoolbooks		
Subjects to Study		
The Teacher		
Chores		
Lunch		

TABLE 5.9   Study the patterns for **new irregular verbs** that you heard in the listening practice above.

begin	**began**	forget	**forgot**	shut	**shut**
break	**broke**	freeze	**froze**	speak	**spoke**
catch	**caught**	hold	**held**	stand	**stood**
choose	**chose**	know	**knew**	strike	**struck**
cost	**cost**	let	**let**	swim	**swam**
draw	**drew**	lose	**lost**	swing	**swung**
drive	**drove**	pay	**paid**	throw	**threw**
fall	**fell**	ride	**rode**	tear	**tore**
feel	**felt**	ring	**rang**	win	**won**
fight	**fought**	run	**ran**	write	**wrote**
find	**found**	say	**said**		

D.   COMPREHENSION

D.1. True or False

Read each statement below about <u>education in the past</u>. Then circle *True* or *False*. If the statement is false, correct it.

1. One teacher taught all the children in the same room.   **True   False**

_____

2. The children had chores to do in the school.   **True   False**

_____

3. When the teacher rang the bell, the children went inside.   **True   False**

_____

4. Children had to attend school for twelve years.   **True   False**

_____

5. Science was an important subject in school.   **True   False**

_____

6. The school provided books and writing materials.   **True   False**

_____

7. The children sat at separate desks in the classroom.   **True   False**

_____

8. The children wrote with chalk on small slates.   **True   False**

_____

9. The three R's were the basic school subjects.   **True   False**

_____

10. The teacher lived in the schoolhouse.   **True   False**

_____

D.2. Comprehension Questions

Now answer these questions about education in the past. Write a complete sentence to answer each question. Follow the patterns in Table 5.9.

1. Why was it difficult to find a good teacher in the past?

   _____

2. Why did teachers think that memorization was important for students?

   _____

3. How did the children help with the work in the schoolhouse?

   _____

4. How was the teacher paid by the townspeople?

   _____

5. Why did many children stop going to school after six years of education?

   _____

TABLE 5.10 **Study the patterns for using can to talk about the past.**

In the 1850s **Could** Yes, they **could**.	students students	**could**	**stay** **stay**	home when the weather was bad. home when the weather was bad?
In the 1850s **Could** No, they **couldn't**.	students students	**couldn't**	**ride** **ride**	a bus to school. a bus to school?

E. ORAL PRACTICE: *IN PAIRS*

Ask questions about education in the present and in the past. Give short answers. Use *can* to talk about education in the present. Use *could* to talk about education in the past. Look for the answers to the questions in your notes in Chart 5.1 on page 133. Take turns asking and answering questions. Follow the models and the patterns in Table 5.10.

MODELS: students / study / science / in school
   Partner A: *Can students study science?*
   Partner B: *Yes, they can.*

   Partner A: *Could they study science in school in the past?*
   Partner B: *No, they couldn't.*

1. students / choose / their subjects / in school
2. students / learn / a foreign language / in school
3. students / use / computers / in school
4. students / buy / a hot meal for lunch / in school
5. students / take / books home / from school
6. students / learn / a foreign language / in school
7. students / ask / questions / in school
8. students / sit / at their own desks / in school

TABLE 5.11 **Study the patterns for using had to to talk about the past.**

Students They	**had to** **didn't have to**	study study	the three R's science	in school. in school.
Did students Yes, they	**have to** **had to**.	memorize	their lessons?	
Did students No, they	**have to** **didn't have to**.	attend school	for twelve years?	

F.   ORAL PRACTICE: *IN PAIRS*

With your partner, ask and answer questions about education in the present and in the past. Use *have to* for the present and *had to* for the past. Look for the answers in your notes on Chart 5.1 on page 133. Follow the models and the patterns in Table 5.11.

MODELS: students / wait / outside / in the morning
       Partner A: *Do students have to wait outside in the morning?*
       Partner B: *No, they don't have to.*
                OR
               No, they don't.
       Partner A: *Did they have to wait outside in the morning in the past?*
       Partner B: *Yes, they had to.*
                OR
               Yes, they did.

       a teacher / go / to college
       Partner A: *Does a teacher have to go to college?*
       Partner B: *Yes, he or she has to.*
                OR
               Yes, he or she does.
       Partner A: *Did a teacher have to go to college in the past?*
       Partner B: *No, he or she didn't have to.*
                OR
               No, he or she didn't.

1. a student / do / chores / in school
2. students / recite / lessons / from memory
3. a student / go / to school / for twelve years
4. students / learn / reading and writing
5. a student / walk / a long distance / to school
6. students / sit / on benches
7. one teacher / teach / in a one-room schoolhouse
8. students / bring / their lunch / from home

TABLE 5.12 Study the patterns for using **would** to talk about **habitual actions in the past**.

One teacher The children	**would** **wouldn't**	**teach** **come**	all the children in one room. to school in bad weather.
Would Yes,	the parents they	**provide** **would**.	meals for the teacher?
Would No,	the students they	**take** **wouldn't**.	books home from school?

G. WRITTEN PRACTICE: *ON YOUR OWN*

Write an answer for each question. Use *would* in your answer to talk about habitual actions in the past. Look for the answers in your notes on Chart 5.1 on page 133. Check your answers with your classmates' answers. Be sure to punctuate your sentences correctly. Follow the model and the patterns in Table 5.12.

MODEL: What would the students do when the teacher rang the bell?

When   *the teacher rang the bell, the students would go inside.*

1. What would the teacher do when a student forgot the lesson?

   When _____

2. Where would the children hang up their coats when they came inside?

   When _____

3. What would the children do when the teacher said the morning prayer?

   When _____

4. What would the children do when the weather was bad?

   When _____

5. What did the students do when they finished school after six years?

   When _____

6. What kind of pen would the teacher use when he or she wanted to write a letter?

   When _____

7. What would the children carry when they came to school in the morning?

   When _____

8. What would the children do when the schoolroom was cold?

   When _____

H. WRITTEN PRACTICE: *ON YOUR OWN*

Write a question for each statement below. Choose a question word or phrase from the list to ask about the underlined part of the statement.

what	where	how much
who	what kind of	how many
when	how	

MODEL: The parents provided meals for the teacher.

Who provided meals for the teacher?

1. The teacher rang the bell in the morning.

_____

2. The older students helped the younger students.

_____

3. The students wrote on a slate.

_____

4. The students learned their lessons by memory.

_____

5. The teacher lived in the people's homes.

_____

6. The students did the chores in the schoolhouse.

_____

7. The students sat on wooden benches.

_____

8. The children played games in the schoolyard.

_____

9. Books cost a lot of money.

_____

10. The parents hired the teacher.

_____

I. ORAL PRACTICE: *WITH YOUR CLASS*

With your class, prepare questions that you can use in an interview with a classmate or a friend to compare education in the past and in the present. Your teacher might ask you to interview an American friend or a classmate from a different country. Discuss with your class the information that you want to ask about. Then write questions to put on the board. Try to write many kinds of questions to use in your interview. Remember to write some questions with *used to, have to, could,* and *would.*

J. WRITTEN PRACTICE: *ON YOUR OWN*

Think about the questions that you wrote with your class. Now write eight questions that you can use in your interview. You can use questions from Exercise I or write new ones.

1. _____
2. _____
3. _____
4. _____
5. _____
6. _____
7. _____
8. _____

K. ORAL PRACTICE: INTERVIEWING

Use your questions from Exercise J to interview a classmate from another country or an American friend. Write down the information that you receive from your interview. Then, report to your class about what you learned in your interview.

L. WRITTEN PRACTICE: *ON YOUR OWN*

Write a report that describes education in the past and education in the present. Use the information you gathered from your interview. Write several sentences about each topic that you asked about.

_____
_____
_____
_____
_____
_____
_____

FIGURE 6.1   The Shapes of Buildings

Architecture

Elements of Architecture
LESSON 1

A.   WARM-UP: *WITH YOUR CLASS*

Look at the shapes on the left. With your class, identify the names of as many shapes as you can.
Write the names in the spaces next to the shapes. Check your answers with your teacher.

B.   DISCUSSION: *WITH YOUR CLASS*

Look at the pictures of buildings on the left. With your class, identify the types of buildings that you
see. What is the function of each building? How old is it? Is it famous? What else do you know
about it? Check your answers with your teacher. Then, discuss the following questions with your
classmates.

1. Which building do you like the most? Why?
2. What do you think is important for an architect to study?
3. Which buildings look similar to buildings in your country?
4. How is modern architecture in your country different from traditional architecture?
5. How are American buildings different from buildings in your country?

C.   FOCUS VOCABULARY: *ON YOUR OWN*

On the lines below, write down any new words that you learn in class. Add to your list as you study
about architecture. Focus on nouns and adjectives.

_____   _____   _____

_____   _____   _____

_____   _____   _____

_____   _____   _____

_____   _____   _____

_____   _____   _____

_____   _____   _____

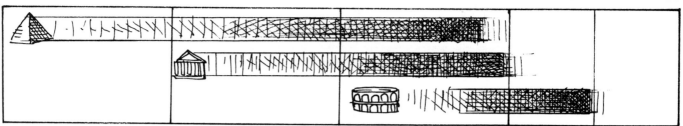

FIGURE 6.2   Architecture Timeline

D. READING   *Great Periods of Architecture*

Introduction to Architecture

From the earliest times in history, people have needed to find shelter. Early people used whatever material they could find in their area to construct buildings where they would be safe from the weather and animals. People learned how to use wood, straw, mud, and stones to make simple buildings that gave them protection. As early civilizations began to develop, people tried to find ways to put up bigger buildings where the king could live or where they could practice their religion or watch sporting events. The first large buildings were palaces, temples, and stadiums.

But it was not easy to find out how to construct large buildings. Probably many first attempts failed when the buildings fell down. People realized that they had to study how to make stronger buildings and how to plan them. Architects are people who know how to plan buildings. Modern architects are capable of building skyscrapers more than one hundred stories high, but they owe their knowledge to the long history of architecture in the Western world.

FIGURE 6.3

Greek Architecture

The ancient Greeks constructed temples that are still famous for their beauty all over the world. The most famous Greek temple is the Parthenon, which the people of Athens constructed almost twenty-five hundred years ago in the fifth century b.c. It has often been used by architects in later centuries as a model for public buildings.

A Greek temple was basically a rectangular box. All around the exterior of the main part of the building, the Greeks set up rounded stone columns which supported the roof of the temple. They designed the roof with a pediment—shaped like a long triangle—at each end so that the two halves of the roof sloped downward.

The method of construction that the Greek architects used is called post and lintel. In this method, the architects first put up two posts and then covered the space at the top with a crossbeam. The posts had to carry all of the weight of the wall and roof above.

The Greeks decorated the pediment, the triangular section under the roof, with statues of their gods. They made the columns out of marble and decorated them with carvings. The three main styles that Greek architects used are still popular in buildings today. They are called *Doric, Ionic,* and *Corinthian.*

Roman Architecture

In the second century B.C., the Romans and the Greeks fought a war which the Romans won. After the Romans conquered Greece, Rome became the most important city in the ancient world. At first, the Romans imitated the Greek style of architecture in many ways, but later they made important discoveries about how to construct bigger buildings.

The greatest architectural invention that the Romans discovered was the use of rounded arches. They found out that an arch made a stronger support than the post and lintel method that the Greeks used. They could put together many arches to make a high semicircular ceiling, which is called a vault. They were able to build arches on top of each other to erect higher walls in buildings. They also knew how to make bridges and aqueducts with arches.

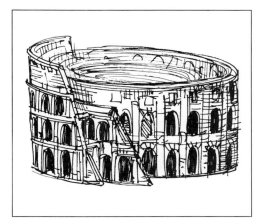

FIGURE 6.4

The Romans liked to construct round buildings like the Colosseum, which was a public stadium. The Pantheon was a large round temple which had a shape like a cylinder. The cylindrical base was covered with a huge dome, another Roman invention.

The Greeks used columns and pediments because they were necessary to support the weight of the building. The Romans used them only for decoration. The arches in the walls carried the real weight of the building. Unlike the Greeks, the Romans built their buildings with bricks and concrete. They often covered the exterior of the building with marble for decoration.

FIGURE 6.5

Architecture in the Middle Ages

After the Roman Empire fell during the third century A.D., architects in the Middle Ages at first continued to follow the Roman style of building. Gradually, a new style developed, especially in the construction of churches in Christian Europe. Usually, the churches had high vaulted ceilings which were made by joining many arches together. Because the arches were rounded like the Roman arches, the style was called Romanesque. The walls were thick in order to support the tall, stone vaults. But the thick walls were not strong enough to hold up the tall, stone ceiling. As a result, the architects needed to construct additional support, which they called a buttress, outside the walls of the church. It was difficult to make windows in the thick walls, so windows were small and the interiors of the churches were dark. Romanesque churches often had towers with cone-shaped steeples at the top.

Gradually, architects learned that if they built the buttress away from the wall and connected it to the wall with half an arch, they could build higher walls and the walls did not have to be thick. The outside supports were called flying buttresses. Also, architects changed the shape of the arch in the interior of the building. When the arch was pointed, it held up the weight better than a rounded arch did. This style was called Gothic. Gothic churches were tall and had pointed arches. Because the walls were not thick and the flying buttresses supported the weight, architects could put in large pointed windows which let light come into the interior. Gothic churches often had towers with very tall, thin spires on top.

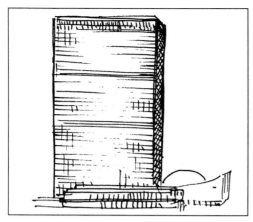

FIGURE 6.6

Modern Architecture

Several other styles were important from the time of the Gothic style until the modern age. During the Renaissance, architects returned to Roman and Greek styles but they often added large domes to their buildings, especially to churches. During the Baroque period, curved lines rather than straight lines were popular. It was not until the end of the nineteenth century that architecture changed significantly and the age of modern architecture began.

Two things happened that led to the modern era of skyscrapers. First, in the middle of the nineteenth century, architects discovered that they could use a steel frame like a skeleton for their buildings. Second, the elevator was invented by Elisha Otis, an American engineer. By the 1880s, architects knew about the possibilities of the electric elevator. Architects could not design a stone building that was taller than eight stories, but when they used a steel frame for the building, they could build much higher. Because stone was not necessary for the walls, architects could cover the exterior with glass windows. The electric elevator made it possible for people to live and work in very tall buildings.

The first skyscraper was built in Chicago in 1884. It was ten stories high. While architects knew that they did not need to use stone or brick to cover the exterior of their new skyscrapers, they thought it was important for decoration. As a result, the early skyscrapers looked heavy. Gradually, architects realized that a skyscraper could be a glass box with nothing on the exterior but glass. Modern skyscrapers became tall geometric forms with glass walls. Now it is not unusual to see skyscrapers that have forty or more stories. The highest skyscraper in the world is the Sears Tower in Chicago. It has 110 stories and is 1,454 feet high.

E.   COMPREHENSION: *ON YOUR OWN*

TABLE 6.1   Study the **new irregular verbs** from the reading.

fall	**fell**	fight	**fought**	win	**won**

E.1. True or False

Read each statement about the reading and then circle *True* or *False*. If the statement is false, correct it.

1. The Romans used concrete as a building material.   **True**   **False**

2. Greek temples were round.   **True**   **False**

3. Renaissance architects invented the dome.   **True**   **False**

4. Steel was discovered in 1884.   **True**   **False**

5. Gothic arches are pointed.   **True**   **False**

6. The Greeks used columns for decoration.   **True**   **False**

7. Romanesque churches had large windows.   **True**   **False**

8. The steel frame allowed architects to build tall skyscrapers.   **True**   **False**

9. The first skyscraper was ten stories high.   **True**   **False**

10. A flying buttress has the shape of half an arch.   **True**   **False**

E.2. Comprehension Questions

Answer the following questions about the reading. Write a complete sentence to answer each question.

1. What kind of buildings did early people probably build first?

2. Why did early people try to build bigger buildings?

3. How did the Romans change architecture?

4. What made it possible for architects to build tall Gothic cathedrals?

5. Why was the invention of the electric elevator important for modern architecture?

TABLE 6.2 **Study the patterns for asking and answering questions** about the past.

Who Elisha Otis	invented	the elevator? the elevator.
Who The Romans	invented	the rounded arch? the rounded arch.
What The pointed arch	was	important in Gothic architecture? important in Gothic architecture.
What Columns	was were	important in Greek architecture? important in Greek architecture.

F.   ORAL PRACTICE: *IN PAIRS*

With your partner, ask and answer questions about the information in the reading. Use *who* and *what* in the questions. Look at the answer clue to find the right question word. Follow the models and the patterns in Table 6.2.

MODELS: _____ / be / popular / with Renaissance architects?
(Domes)
      Partner A: *What was popular with Renaissance architects?*
      Partner B: *Domes were popular with Renaissance architects.*

_____ / construct / bridges with arches?
(The Romans)
      Partner A: *Who constructed bridges with arches?*
      Partner B: *The Romans constructed bridges with arches.*

1. _____ / build / the Parthenon?
   (The ancient Greeks)

2. _____ / hold up / the roof of a Greek temple?
   (Columns)

3. _____ / decorate / the temple pediment with statues?
   (Greek sculptors)

4. _____ / be / between the posts on top?
   (A lintel)

5. _____ / conquer / Greece / in the second century B.C.?
   (The Romans)

6. _____ / support / the weight / in a Roman temple?
   (Arches)

7. _____ / be / difficult / to make / in a thick wall?
   (Windows)

8. _____ / be / stronger / than a rounded arch?
   (A pointed arch)

9. _____ / put / large windows / in the wall?
   (Gothic architects)

10. _____ / copied / Roman and Greek styles?
    (Renaissance architects)

11. _____ / use / glass / for exterior walls?
    (Modern architects)

12. _____ / carry / the weight / in the first skyscraper?
    (A steel frame)

G. WRITTEN PRACTICE: *ON YOUR OWN*

Use the question words below to write questions and answers about architecture in the past.

what	where	what kind of
who	how	which
when	how many	why

Use the pronouns *it* or *they* in the answer when possible. The answer clues are in parentheses. Follow the models.

MODELS: Gothic buildings / have / _____ windows

   What kind of windows did Gothic buildings have?

   (pointed)

   They had pointed windows.

   the column in a Greek temple / support / _____

   What did the column in a Greek temple support?

   (the roof)

   They supported the roof.

1. early architects / use / _____ / to construct buildings

_____

   (materials from their area)

_____

2. early people / build / _____ buildings / for shelter

_____

   (simple)

_____

3. the most beautiful Greek temple / be / _____

    _____

    (the Parthenon)

    _____

4. Greek temples / have / a _____ shape

    _____

    (rectangular)

    _____

5. Greek architects / put up / columns / _____

    _____

    (around the exterior of the temple)

    _____

6. there / be / _____ styles of Greek columns

    _____

    (three)

    _____

7. the Romans / can / make / high ceilings / _____

    _____

    (by putting together arches)

    _____

8. the Romans / like / to construct / _____ buildings

    _____

    (round)

    _____

9. the Roman Empire / fall / _____

    _____

    (in the third century A.D.)

    _____

10. architects in the Middle Ages / imitate / _____

_____

   (the Romans)

_____

11. Romanesque walls / be / thick / because _____

_____

   (they supported a tall vault)

_____

12. the flying buttresses / be / _____

_____

   (on the exterior of the church)

_____

13. modern architecture / begin / _____

_____

   (at the end of the nineteenth century)

_____

14. the first skyscraper / be / _____ stories high

_____

   (ten)

_____

TABLE 6.3   Study the patterns for **combining sentences with which and that.**

An aqueduct is a structure.		It carries water to a city.
An aqueduct is a structure	**which** **that**	carries water to a city.
A Greek temple had columns.		They held up the roof.
A Greek temple had columns	**which** **that**	held up the roof.

H. ORAL PRACTICE: *WITH YOUR CLASS*

Using complete sentences, take turns explaining or describing the words below. Choose a phrase from the list for each sentence. Use *which* or *that* to combine the two parts of your sentence. Follow the model and the patterns in Table 6.3.

has pointed arches
holds up the roof
can be many stories high
teaches how to plan buildings
has a circular base

carries water to a city
supports the weight of a skyscraper
uses rounded arches
is on the outside wall of a building

MODEL: Architecture (a science)
        *Architecture is a science **which** teaches how to plan buildings.*

1. A skyscraper (building)
2. Gothic architecture (style)
3. An aqueduct (structure)
4. A column (post)

5. Romanesque architecture (style)
6. A steel frame (skeleton)
7. A buttress (kind of support)
8. A dome (rounded roof)

TABLE 6.4 **Study the patterns for combining sentences with which and that.**

The Parthenon is a temple.		The ancient Greeks built it.
The Parthenon is a temple	**which** **that**	the ancient Greeks built.
The Romans invented the rounded arch.		They used it to make tall walls.
The Romans invented the rounded arch	**which** **that**	they used to make tall walls.

I. ORAL PRACTICE: *WITH YOUR CLASS*

Using complete sentences, take turns describing or explaining the words below. Choose a phrase from the list for each sentence. Use *which* or *that* to combine the two parts of your sentence. Follow the model and the patterns in Table 6.4.

early people built it for protection
the Greeks used it for building
artists carved it for statues
architects started to use it in the nineteenth Century
Gothic architects first designed it

ancient Greeks built it in Athens
the Romans built it for sports
the Romans invented it
Elisha Otis invented it

MODEL: an elevator (machine)
        *An elevator is a machine **which** Elisha Otis invented.*

1. the Parthenon (a temple)
2. rounded arch (type of construction)
3. a shelter (structure)
4. the Coliseum (a stadium)

5. post and lintel (method of construction)
6. marble (kind of stone)
7. a flying buttress (a kind of support)
8. steel (a building material)

J. WRITTEN PRACTICE: *On Your Own*

J.1. Sentence Combining

Use the cue words below to make a new sentence. Combine the two parts of your sentence with *which* or *that*. Check your answers with your classmates' answers.

MODELS: The Romans / build / aqueducts /
                    the aqueducts / carry / water to the cities

> *The Romans built aqueducts which carried water to the cities.*

Romanesque buildings / have / walls
the walls / be / thick

> *Romanesque buildings had walls that were thick.*

1. Renaissance architects / like / to build / churches
   the churches / have / domes

   _____

2. Gothic architects / like / to build / towers
   the towers / have / thin spires

   _____

3. Romanesque architects / use / arches
   the arches / be / rounded

   _____

4. Greek architects / use / columns
   the columns / hold up / the roof

   _____

5. Before the twentieth century, architects / design / stone buildings
   the stone buildings / be / only eight stories high

   _____

6. In 1884, an architect / plan / a skyscraper
   the skyscraper / be / ten stories high

   _____

J.2. Sentence Combining

Use the cue words below to make a sentence. Combine the two parts of your sentence with *which* or *that*. Check your answers with your classmates' answers.

MODEL   The Greeks and the Romans / fight / a war
            the Romans / win / it

The Greeks and the Romans fought a war which the Romans won.

1. The Romanesque architects / use / a rounded arch
   the Romans / invent / it

   _____

2. The Gothic architects / invent / a pointed arch
   they / use / it / for making tall vaults

   _____

3. Renaissance architects / design / domes
   they / put / them / on churches

   _____

4. The Romans / invent / concrete
   they / use / it / as a building material

   _____

5. Otis / invent / the elevator
   architects / need / it / for tall skyscrapers

   _____

6. Nineteenth-century architects / construct / a steel frame
   they / cover / it / with stone

   _____

K.   ORAL PRACTICE: *IN SMALL GROUPS*

Take turns describing the buildings in the pictures in Figure 6.7. The person who is describing the building can talk only about the building's shapes and its style. After the person says four sentences to describe the building, the other members of the group should try to guess which building it is. Then, the next person describes a different building.

Taj Mahal	Hagia Sophia
Empire State Building	Pyramid Building in San Francisco
Chinese pagoda	Japanese temple
St. Peter's Basilica	St. Paul's Cathedral in London
Great Pyramid of Giza	Mayan pyramid
Notre Dame in Paris	St. Patrick's Cathedral in New York City
John Hancock Center, Chicago	Citicorp Tower, New York City

Figure 6.7

L. WRITTEN PRACTICE: *ON YOUR OWN*

Choose one of the pairs of buildings from Exercise K. Write a description of the two buildings. Explain what is the same and what is different in the buildings. Try to use *which* or *that* to combine sentences.

_____

_____

_____

_____

_____

_____

_____

Construction
LESSON 2

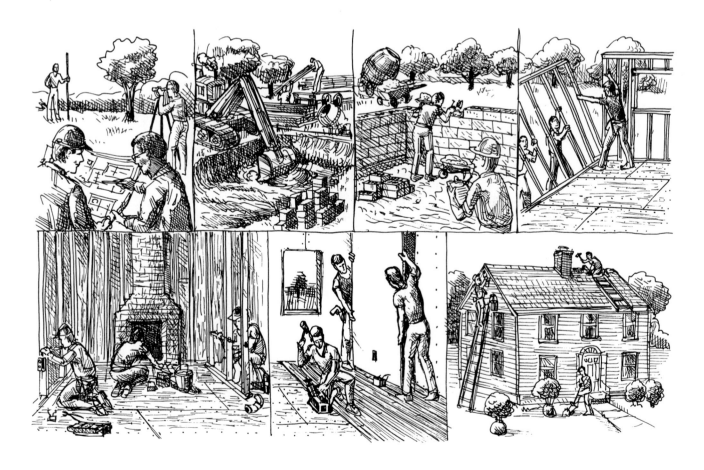

FIGURE 6.8   Construction of a house

A. WARM-UP: *WITH YOUR CLASS*

Look at the pictures in Figure 6.8 showing the construction of a modern house. With your classmates, describe what is happening in each picture. Name the parts of the house and the materials that the builders are using. Check your answers with your teacher.

B. DISCUSSION: *WITH YOUR CLASS*

Take turns asking and answering these questions.

1. How is this house similar to houses in your country?
2. How is it different from houses in your country?
3. Why is a foundation important?
4. What is the traditional building material for houses in your country?
5. Would you choose to live in a house that is modern in style or traditional in style?

C. FOCUS VOCABULARY: *ON YOUR OWN*

On the lines below, write down any new words that you learn in class. Add to your list as you study about the construction of buildings. Focus on nouns and verbs.

_____ _____ _____

_____ _____ _____

_____ _____ _____

_____ _____ _____

_____ _____ _____

TABLE 6.5   Study the patterns for talking about **continuous actions in the past.**

What	**was**	the surveyor **doing**?
He	**was measuring**	the area for the house.
What	**were**	the carpenters **doing**?
They	**were erecting**	the wooden frame.

D. ORAL PRACTICE: *WITH YOUR CLASS*

Using the cue words, ask and answer questions about continuous actions in the past. Look for the activities in the pictures in Exercise A.. Follow the models and the patterns in Table 6.5.

MODELS: contractor / inspect the work
        Student A: *What was the contractor doing?*
        Student B: *The contractor was inspecting the work.*

        masons / build the foundation wall
        Student A: *What were the masons doing?*
        Student B: *The masons were building the foundation wall.*

1. the architect / plan the design
2. the surveyor / measure the area
3. the laborers / mix the concrete
4. the bulldozer / dig the foundation hole
5. the workers / prepare the mortar
6. the mason / place the bricks together
7. the builders / erect the frame
8. the truck / deliver the boards
9. the workers / put up the walls
10. the roofers / put on the roof
11. the workers / construct the house
12. the architect / watch the progress
13. the plumber / install the pipes
14. the electrician / put in the electric wires
15. the painters / paint the exterior
16. the landscapers / plant trees

E. LISTENING PRACTICE: *On Your Own*

While your teacher is telling you about the construction of the Great Pyramid, listen and take notes. Write the information under each section. In some cases, you'll need to listen for specific facts. In other cases, you can listen for general information. After each section, check your notes with your classmates and fill in the labels in the drawings.

Introduction
Description of a Pyramid

Shape _____

Pyramids of Egypt

Who _____

When _____

Why _____

Religion _____

The Great Pyramid

When _____

Name of the Pharaoh _____

Where _____

Mystery of the Great Pyramid _____

Why a Mystery _____

Getting Ready For Construction
Planning the Pyramid

Architect _____

_____

Assistants _____

_____

Figure 6.9   Construction of the Great Pyramid

Preparation for Building _____

_____

Architect's Duties _____

_____

Finding the Workers

Definition of Craftsmen _____

_____

Kinds of Craftsmen _____

_____

_____

_____

_____

Definition of Laborer _____

_____

Kind of Work _____

_____

How Many Workers _____

First Activities

1st _____

2nd _____

3rd _____

Stone Cutters in the Quarry

Job of the Scribe _____

Job of the Stone Cutters _____

Where _____

Weight of Stone Blocks _____

Delivering the Stone Blocks

How _____

Where _____

Taking the Stone Blocks to the Pyramid Site

Gang _____

Foreman _____

How _____

_____

_____

Construction of the Pyramid

The Foundation

When _____

1st Step _____

The Base

Size _____

1st Step _____

2nd Step _____

Building the Levels of the Pyramid

Description of Ramps _____

How Many at First _____

Where _____

How Many Later _____

Why _____

How Many Blocks a Day _____

The Capstone

Description _____

What Level _____

Ceremony _____

Finishing the Pyramid

Polishing the Surface of the Pyramid

Two Activities _____

_____

Scaffold _____

Where _____

Height _____

Workers' Job _____

Completion of the Pyramid

Height _____

Number of Stone Blocks _____

Number of Workers _____

Number of Years _____

F.   ORAL PRACTICE: *WITH YOUR CLASS*

Your teacher will ask you to make an oral summary of a section of the notes you took about the Great Pyramid in Exercise E. With your notes, report what was happening in your section of the story. Use complete sentences. Review the patterns for talking about continuous actions in the past in Table 6.5.

G.   COMPREHENSION: *ON YOUR OWN*

G.1. True or False

Read each statement about the reading and then circle *True* or *False*. If the statement is false, correct it.

1. We know exactly how the Egyptians built the pyramids.   **True**   **False**

   _____

2. The Great Pyramid was a palace for the pharaoh.   **True**   **False**

   _____

3. The construction of the Great Pyramid took thirty years.   **True**   **False**

   _____

4. Boats brought the stone blocks to the building site.   **True**   **False**

   _____

5. The workers came from the city by boat every day.   **True**   **False**

   _____

6. The stone blocks weighed about 2,000 pounds each.   **True**   **False**

   _____

7. The capstone was the final level of construction.   **True**   **False**

8. The workers polished the stones of each layer before they started
   to make the next layer.   **True**   **False**

9. The workers used horses to pull the stones up the ramps.   **True**   **False**

10. The workers could move 500 blocks a day.   **True**   **False**

G.2. Comprehension Questions

Answer the following questions, using the information in the lecture and your own knowledge. Write a complete sentence to answer each question.

1. Why did the ancient Egyptians construct the pyramids?

2. Why was construction of the pyramids slow?

3. Why did the architect have to be a good organizer?

4. Why were ramps necessary?

5. Why do people still think the pyramids are special buildings?

TABLE 6.6 **Study the patterns for combining sentences with who or that.**

The architect had a scribe.		The scribe wrote down the list of materials.
The architect had a scribe	**who** **that**	wrote down the list of materials.
The foreman was a person.		He organized the workers.
The foreman was a person	**who** **that**	organized the workers.

H. ORAL PRACTICE: *WITH YOUR CLASS*

Using complete sentences, take turns talking about people who worked on the pyramid. Use the phrases below to explain what the person (or people) did. Follow the models and the patterns in Table 6.6.

cut the stone in the quarry
measure the size of the site
design the pyramid
say prayers
pull and push the sleds

write the list of materials
inspect the work
made the wooden sleds and tools
polish the stone blocks
have skilled jobs

MODELS: architect
> *The architect was the person* **who** *designed the pyramid.*

craftsmen
> *The craftsmen were the people* **who** *had skilled jobs.*

1. the surveyor
2. the priests
3. the foreman
4. the carpenter

5. the masons
6. the stone cutter
7. the scribe
8. the laborers

I. WRITTEN PRACTICE: *ON YOUR OWN*

Write a sentence to explain each kind of activity given in the cue words below. Choose the name of the workers from this list. Follow the models and the patterns in Table 6.6.

architect   foreman   carpenter   priests
mason   laborers   ramp builders   craftsmen
surveyor   scribes   stone cutters

MODELS: make / the plan for the pyramid

> *The architect was the person who made the plan for the pyramid.*

have / special jobs

> *The craftsmen were the people who had special jobs.*

1. measure / the area of the pyramid

2. know / how to put the blocks together

3. work / together in a gang

4. build / wooden sleds

_____

5. prepare / the stone blocks in the quarry

_____

6. keep / lists of all the materials

_____

7. conduct / the religious ceremonies

_____

8. be / the leader of the gang

_____

9. construct and repair / the ramps

_____

10. have / skilled jobs

_____

J. WRITTEN PRACTICE: *ON YOUR OWN*

Write a sentence to combine each pair of cue words below. Follow the model and the patterns in Table 6.6.

MODEL: The boats / deliver / the stone blocks
          the workers / need / them / at the construction site

   The boats delivered the stone blocks _____

which *the workers needed at the construction site.* _____

1. The pyramid / have / four triangular sides
   they / meet / in a point / at the top

_____

which _____

2. The workers / live / in a small town
   they / construct / it / near the pyramid

_____

which _____

3. Cheops / be / the pharaoh
   he / build / the Great Pyramid

_____

who _____

4. The foreman / be / the leader
   he / tell / the laborers / what to do

_____

who _____

5. The workers / clear away / the sand
   it / cover / the solid rock

_____

which _____

6. The pharaoh / approve / the design
   the architect / make / it

_____

which _____

7. The stone blocks / come / from quarries
   they / be / far away / from the pyramid

_____

which _____

8. The craftsmen / be / the workers
   they / have / special skills

_____

who _____

TABLE 6.7 **Study the patterns for using while to talk about two continuous actions in the past.**

The laborers **were pulling** the sleds. The ramp builders **were pouring** oil on the road.
The laborers **were pulling** the sleds **while** the ramp builders **were pouring** oil on the road.
OR
While the ramp builders **were pouring** oil on the road, the laborers *were pulling* the sleds.

K. WRITTEN PRACTICE: *On Your Own*

Write a sentence with the following cue words showing that two actions were happening at the same time in the past. Follow the models and the patterns in Table 6.7.

MODEL   the stone cutters / cut / new blocks of stone
                   the workers / load / them / on the boat

The stone cutters were cutting new blocks of stone **while**
the workers were loading them on the boats.

OR

While *the workers were loading new blocks of stone on the boats,*
the stone cutters were cutting them.

1. the architect / plan / the design / for the pyramid
    the priests / choose / the site

While _____

_____

2. the workers / set up / temporary towns
    the architect / order / stones / from the quarry

_____ **while**

_____

3. some workers / unload / the stones / from the boats
    other workers / pull / the stones / to the pyramid

While _____

_____

4. the workers / lay / the stones / in place
    the foreman / check / their work

_____ **while**

_____

5. some workers / pull / the stones / with ropes
    other workers / push / them / with poles

_____ **while**

_____

6. the architect / direct / the construction
   the pharaoh / watch / the progress

While _____

_____

7. workers / drag / stones / up the ramp
   other workers / bring / the empty sleds / down the ramp

_____ **while**

_____

8. the priests / say / prayers
   the workers / install / the capstone

While _____

_____

TABLE 6.8   Study the patterns for using **when** and **while** to talk **about two actions in the past**.

The workers **were pulling** the block of stone **when** the rope **broke**. The rope **broke while** the workers **were pulling** the block of stone.

L.   WRITTEN PRACTICE: *ON YOUR OWN*

Combine each pair of sentences, using *when* or *while*. Do not change the order of the sentences. Follow the model and the patterns in Table 6.8.

MODEL: The workers were working. The pharaoh arrived.

   The workers were working when the pharaoh arrived. _____

1. The workers were preparing the site. The architect finished his plan.

_____

2. The rope broke. The workers were pulling the sled.

_____

3. The sun was coming up. The work started.

_____

4. The scribe was waiting in the landing area. The boats brought materials.

_____

5. The workers brought the stone blocks. The masons were getting the mortar ready.

_____

6. The workers installed the capstone. The priests were singing.

_____

7. The workers were clearing away the sand. The surveyor measured the base.

_____

8. The boats came to the landing area. The workers were waiting.

_____

M. WRITTEN PRACTICE: *ON YOUR OWN*

Write questions and answers about the construction of the Great Pyramid. Use the cue words for your questions. Follow the model.

<u>MODEL:</u>   what / the surveyor / do

During the construction of the pyramid, ___*what did the surveyor do?*___

___*He measured the area of the pyramid.*___

1. what / the mason / do

During the construction of the pyramid, _____

_____ ?

_____ .

2. what / the scribe / do

During the construction of the pyramid, _____

_____ ?

_____ .

3. what / the pharaoh / do

While the workers were constructing the pyramid, _____

_____ ?

_____ .

4. what / the priests / do

While the workers were putting in the capstone, _____

_____ ?

_____ .

5. what / the foremen / do

During the construction of the pyramid, _____

_____ ?

_____ .

6. what / the ramp builders / do

During the construction of the pyramid, _____

_____ ?

_____ .

Architecture of the Future

LESSON 3

FIGURE 6.10

A. WARM-UP: *WITH YOUR CLASS*

Look at the pictures of buildings in Figure 6.10 which show how people might live and work in the future. What elements in the pictures look like architecture of the future? Why?

B. DISCUSSION: *WITH YOUR CLASS*

Discuss these questions with your classmates.

1. What will be different in houses of the future?
2. How will cities be different in the future?
3. What are the factors that will influence the way people will live in the future?
4. How can architects build buildings that will save energy in the future?
5. Where will architects find new places for building? In the ocean? Underground? In space?

C. FOCUS VOCABULARY: *ON YOUR OWN*

On the lines below, write down new words that you learn in class. Add to your list as you study about buildings in the future. Focus on nouns and adjectives.

_____   _____   _____

_____   _____   _____

_____   _____   _____

_____   _____   _____

TABLE 6.9   Study the patterns for talking about **actions in the future**.

Houses will	have	computerized systems	in the future.
Houses will not	have	many windows	in the future.
Will people	live	under glass domes	in the future?
Yes, they will.			
No, they won't.			

D. ORAL PRACTICE: *IN SMALL GROUPS*

Ask and answer questions about possible ways that architecture will change in the future. Answer with your own opinion. Explain why you think an idea will or will not be possible. When you finish, discuss your opinions with your class. Follow the model and the patterns in Table 6.9.

MODEL: on the moon

Student A: *Will people live on the moon in the future?*
Student B: *Yes, they will. People will build cities on the moon.*

OR

No, they won't. People will not be able to live on the moon.

1. under the ocean
2. in skyscraper cities
3. under a glass dome
4. at the North Pole
5. in space stations
6. in solar-heated houses
7. inside a mountain
8. underground
9. on a different planet
10. in a computerized house

E. READING *Architecture in the Future*

Architects know that they must design buildings that will be useful now and also in the future. But how can they know what will happen ten years, fifty years, or one hundred years from now? By studying people's needs and problems, architects can make plans for buildings that will be adaptable to the needs of people in the future. The needs of society will shape the way architects design buildings for future use.

The Problems of the Cities

The world's population is increasing. In the year 2000 there will be more than six billion people on earth. More and more people are living in the world's cities. Big cities are becoming bigger. In some areas, such as the East Coast of the United States, urban growth has increased so much that experts talk about the *megapolis*, one large belt of urban area from Boston to Washington, D.C. Will there be enough land for all of the people who want to live in the cities?

As the population increases and the cities become more and more crowded, architects will have to try to find a solution for the lack of space and the increased number of people. Because there will be less and less available land for building, the cost of land will become more and more expensive. Architects will need to make buildings that will be able to hold a large number of people on a small amount of land. Will the solution be to build taller skyscrapers in big cities?

Mile-high Skyscrapers

Some architects who are planning for the future think that the solution will be to build mile-high skyscrapers. They are designing skyscrapers that will be one or two miles high, so more people will be able to work and live in one building. The skyscrapers will be self-supporting systems. The people will live and work in the same building. All of the services that people need, such as stores, banks, schools, and entertainment will be available in the same building. People will not have to go out to find what they need. People will not have to commute to work from their homes. In that way, they will save energy. Because a great number of people will live in one tall building, the tall skyscraper will save land space, too. Perhaps the people of the future will live in self-supporting skyscraper communities instead of in cities.

The Energy Crisis

The problem of pollution from burning fossil fuels and the rising cost of energy will affect the possibilities that architects will have. A tall skyscraper requires energy for heating and air conditioning, and electricity for lighting and elevators. It may not be advisable to build tall skyscrapers in the future. The cost of the energy that the skyscrapers will require could make them economically impossible.

Buildings with Alternative Energy

Other architects are thinking of buildings that will use less energy. Perhaps solar energy will replace energy from fossil fuels. In order to use solar energy, buildings in the future will need to have solar collectors on the roof and large windows. Houses will have many large windows on the southern side so that the sun's heat will enter the house, but there will be few windows on the other sides of the house.

Another way to save energy is to build houses that will look like small hills. These houses are called earth-sheltered houses. They will have one wall that is visible, and the other walls and the roof will be inside the hill. This construction will keep heat inside the house and will require less energy. In the summer, the earth around the house will keep the interior cool.

Future Style

Besides the problems of energy and space, architects are thinking of future styles. Some architects predict that future buildings will look very functional. They say that buildings do not need decoration. In their opinion, future buildings will be simple and practical.

On the other hand, there are architects who think that decoration is important. They want to build buildings that people will think are attractive. One style that might become more important in the future is postmodernism. The postmodernist architects feel that people are tired of glass skyscrapers which look similar to each other. Postmodernists will build buildings that use many geometric forms, so the buildings will look more interesting.

Other Possibilities

There are other possibilities for the future, too. Perhaps cities will be underground, so they will conserve energy and resources. Maybe cities will have large domes that will cover everything and control the climate. It is possible that people will live in houses under the ocean. And no one knows whether or not human beings will be living on the moon, on other planets, or on space stations in the near future.

F. COMPREHENSION: *ON YOUR OWN*

F.1. True or False

Read each statement about the reading and then circle *True* or *False*. If the statement is false, correct it.

1. Architecture will change in the future.   **True**   **False**

_____

2. Fossil energy will not be expensive.   **True**   **False**

_____

3. Underground living is a possibility for the future.   **True**   **False**

_____

4. Postmodernists will design functional buildings.   **True**   **False**

_____

5. Solar houses will have windows on the northern wall.   **True**   **False**

_____

6. Architects are already planning for the future.   **True**   **False**

_____

7. People in skyscraper communities will not have to commute to work.   **True**   **False**

8. Skyscrapers are not good energy savers.   **True**   **False**

9. A functional building has a lot of decoration.   **True**   **False**

10. Cities will become more crowded.   **True**   **False**

F.2. Comprehension Questions

Answer the following questions about the reading. Write a complete sentence to answer each question.

1. How will architects make decisions about designing buildings for the future?

2. Why do skyscrapers require a lot of energy?

3. Why will solar energy become more important for the future?

4. What kind of buildings will postmodernists build?

5. How will the growth in population affect architecture?

TABLE 6.10 **Study the patterns for there will be.**

	There	will	be	cities underground in the future.
Will	there		be	cities under the ocean in the future?
	Yes, there will. Yes, there will be.			
	No, there won't. No, there won't be.			

G. ORAL PRACTICE: *IN PAIRS*

With your partner, ask and answer questions about the future. Use the information in the reading or your own knowledge to answer the questions. Add a sentence to explain why you think your answer is correct. Check your answers with your classmates' answers. Follow the models and the patterns in Table 6.10.

MODELS: fossil fuel / be / cheap / in the future
        Partner A: *Will fossil fuel be cheap in the future?*
        Partner B: *No, it won't be because there will not be enough of it.*
                    OR
            Yes, it will be because companies will find more oil.

        cities / become / overpopulated
        Partner A: *Will cities become overpopulated?*
        Partner B: *Yes, cities will become overpopulated because the world's population is increasing.*
                    OR
            No, cities won't become overpopulated because there will be cities underground, under the ocean, and in space.

1. there / be / a city on the moon
2. architects / build / small houses
3. there / be / new kinds of energy
4. there / be / solar collectors / on buildings
5. people / like / to live underground
6. an earth-sheltered house / save / energy
7. a glass dome / control / the climate
8. skyscrapers / become / taller and taller
9. people / build / traditional houses
10. there / be / cities / under the ocean

TABLE 6.11   Study the patterns for **asking questions** about the future.

People	will	live on the moon.
Where	will people	live?
Overpopulation		will create problems.
What		will create problems?

H. ORAL PRACTICE: *IN SMALL GROUPS*

Take turns asking and answering questions about architecture and living in the future. Use *will* in your questions and answers. Follow the models and the patterns in Table 6.11.

MODELS: what / become / more expensive
        fossil fuel
        Student A: *What will become more expensive in the future?*
        Student B: *Fossil fuel will become more expensive.*

        what kind / heat / houses in the future / use
        solar heat
        Student A: *What kind of heat will houses in the future use?*
        Student B: *They will use solar heat.*

1. what / postmodernist architects / build
   buildings with geometric shapes
2. what kind / buildings / functional architects / design
   simple buildings

3. how tall / skyscraper communities / be
more than one mile high
4. what kind / house / look / like a hill
an earth-sheltered house
5. where / solar-heated house / have / windows
on the southern wall
6. when / there / be / a city / on the moon
in the twenty-first century
7. what / control / the climate / of a city
a glass dome
8. how many / people / there / be / in the year 2000
more than six billion
9. where / architects / find / more space / for building
underground and under the ocean
10. where / people / live / in space
on space stations

I. WRITTEN PRACTICE: *ON YOUR OWN*

Write a question to ask about the underlined words in each statement below. Begin each question with a question word. Follow the model.

MODEL: People will conserve energy <u>by living underground</u>.

How will people conserve energy?

1. Architects will build glass domes <u>over the cities</u>.

_____

2. People will live on <u>space stations</u> in space.

_____

3. Skyscrapers will be <u>two or three miles</u> high.

_____

4. Earth-sheltered houses will look like <u>hills</u>.

_____

5. <u>People who live in skyscraper communities</u> will not have to commute to work.

_____

6. <u>Solar collectors</u> will store the sun's heat.

_____

7. Scientists will find a way to control <u>the environment</u>.

_____

8. People in skyscrapers will <u>never</u> have to go outside.

_____

9. Cities will run out of <u>building space</u>.

_____

10. Architects will have to develop new kinds of housing <u>in the future</u>.

_____

TABLE 6.12 **Study the patterns for talking about continuous actions in the future.**

People will	be using	solar energy	in the twenty-first century.
Will people	be using	solar energy	in the twenty-first century?

Yes, they will be.
Yes, they will.

No, they won't be / will not be.
No, they won't / will not.

J. ORAL PRACTICE: *WITH YOUR CLASS*

Ask and answer the questions below about the future. Use the patterns for talking about continuous actions in the future. Find the answers in the information in the reading, or express your own opinion. Follow the model and the patterns in Table 6.12.

MODEL: where / people / live / in the twenty-first century
        Student A: *Where will people be living in the twenty-first century?*
        Student B: *They will be living underground.*

1. Where will people in skyscraper communities be working?
2. Why will cities be growing larger?
3. What kind of houses will architects be designing?
4. What kind of energy will people be using in their houses?
5. How many people will be living on earth in the year 2000?
6. Where will architects be trying to construct cities?
7. What will be controlling the environment in cities?
8. Where will people be living in space?
9. Which architects will be designing buildings with geometric forms?
10. When will space stations be traveling in space?

TABLE 6.13 **Study the patterns for using when to talk about two actions in the future.**

Fossil fuel will become more expensive.
People will use electric cars.
When fossil fuel becomes more expensive, people **will use** electric cars.

K.   ORAL PRACTICE: *WITH YOUR CLASS*

Use the statements below to ask questions. Use *what will happen* to start your question. With your classmates, give more than one possible answer for each question. Use the information in the reading, or give your own opinion. Follow the model and the patterns in Table 6.13.

MODEL: Space travel will become possible.
Student A: *What will happen when space travel becomes possible?*
Student B: *When space travel becomes possible, people will live on space stations.*
Student C: *When space travel becomes possible, there will be cities on the moon.*

1. Cities will become overcrowded.
2. There will not be enough land.
3. Architects will build solar-heated houses.
4. A glass dome will control the environment.
5. The world supply of fossil fuel will run out.
6. A skyscraper community will be self-supporting.
7. Skyscrapers will all look the same.
8. Architects will study people's needs and problems.

L.   WRITTEN PRACTICE: *ON YOUR OWN*

Write new sentences about future actions using the words below. Use *when* to start your sentence. Follow the model.

MODEL: there / be / cities / underground
people / conserve / natural resources

When there are cities underground, people will conserve natural resources.

1. fossil fuel / be / unavailable
people / use / alternative energy

_____

2. cities / become / overcrowded
land / be / very expensive

_____

3. people / use / solar energy
they / reduce / air pollution

_____

4. architects / plan / for the future
they / design / new kinds of buildings

_____

5. it / be / possible / to travel in space
people / live / on space stations

_____

6. the earth / become / overpopulated
people / look for / new places / to live

_____

M. ORAL PRACTICE: *IN SMALL GROUPS*

Look at Figure 6.12 of architecture for the future. With your group use complete sentences to describe the elements of each kind of building. Remember that the buildings are for the future, so you will have to use *will* in your sentences. Try to use a variety of sentence structures.

MODEL:

In the future, architects will build houses…
The houses will…

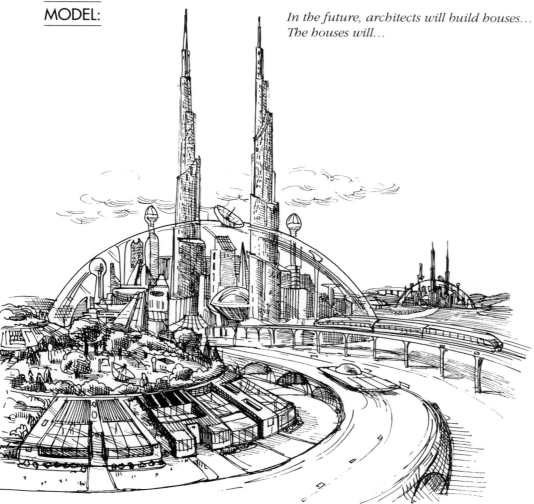

FIGURE 6.12

N. WRITTEN PRACTICE: *ON YOUR OWN*

Write your own sentences about one of the buildings in Exercise M. Use the sentences from your group, or write new ones. Use *will* in your sentences.

_____

_____

_____

FIGURE 7.1   Stressful Situations

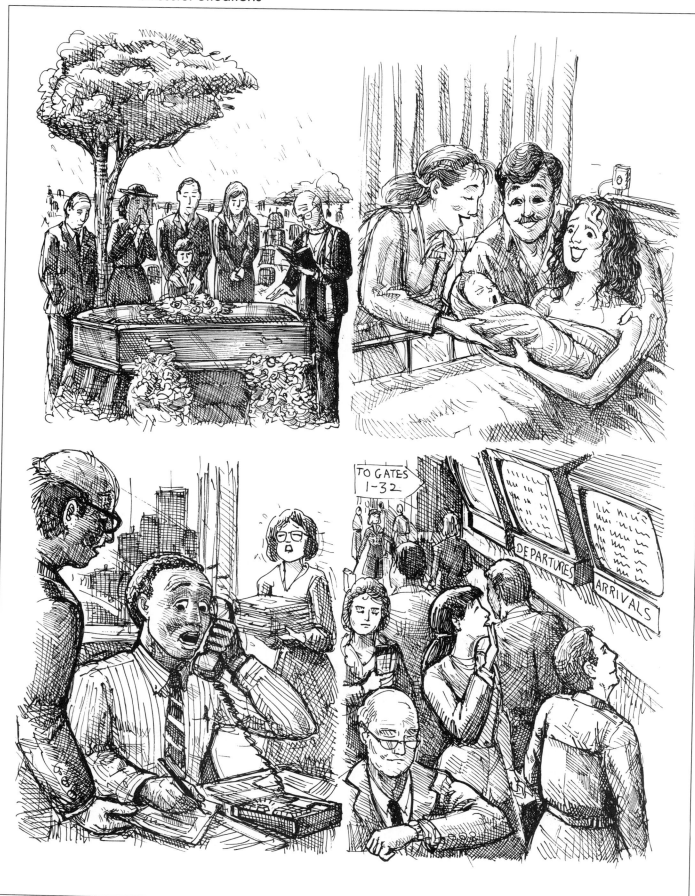

Stress
CHAPTER 7

Causes of Stress
LESSON 1

A. WARM-UP: *WITH YOUR CLASS*

Look at the pictures in Figure 7.1. What has happened to the people in the pictures? How do you think they feel? Anxious? Happy? Sad? Discuss your ideas with your classmates.

B. DISCUSSION: *WITH YOUR CLASS*

Discuss these questions with your classmates.

1. What is stress?
2. What can cause stress in your life?
3. Do you feel stress today? What event is causing your stress?
4. Have you experienced more or less stress since you arrived in the United States?
5. How important is it for you to take quiet time for yourself every day?
6. What kinds of stressful situations do you think that international students experience the most?

C. CLASSIFYING: *IN SMALL GROUPS AND WITH YOUR CLASS*

Look at the following list of factors associated with stress among international students. Which of these factors have you experienced? Do you agree that these factors cause stress? Can you think of other things that might cause stress? In your group, try to classify the items on the list into categories. Use the following chart. Then, compare your chart with those of other groups. Discuss similarities and differences.

- language difficulties
- differences in values
- different food
- climate changes
- different educational system
- discrimination against your nationality or cultural group
- loneliness, isolation
- missing family members and friends
- money problems
- difficulty in finding an affordable place to live
- uncertainty about future acceptance at a university
- unfamiliar health-care system

- _____
- _____
- _____

CHART 7.1

Emotional Factors	Cultural Factors	Educational Factors	Other

D. FOCUS VOCABULARY: *ON YOUR OWN*

On the lines below, write the new words that you learn in class. Add to your list as you study the causes of stress. Focus on new verbs and adjectives.

_____   _____   _____

_____   _____   _____

_____   _____   _____

_____   _____   _____

_____   _____   _____

E. READING

Stress

What is stress?

Stress is a term without an exact meaning. It usually is used to describe a physical or emotional reaction to an event or situation that we can't deal with well. Usually we cope, or deal with, the events of our lives well, but sometimes our systems for coping break down and we experience stress.

Causes of stress

Everyone has experienced stress. Almost everything we do causes some level of stress. If you have ever been in a hurry for an appointment, you have experienced stress. If you have gotten married, had children, gotten jobs, or been promoted, you have experienced stress. Similarly, if you have ever been fired, lost your luggage, gotten divorced, or lost a family member to death, you have experienced stress. Stress is usually a normal part of your everyday life, and you usually have the ability to cope with these things. Stress can come from happy or unhappy events and situations. Usually stress does not continue for a long time. Once the situation or event has ended, the stress also ends. While you may not like feeling stress, you would not want to be completely stress-free. In fact, it has been said that the absence of stress is death.

Chronic stress

Stress becomes a problem only when so many stressful conditions exist that you don't have much time to relax between them. This is called *chronic stress*. If chronic stress continues for a long time, serious physical and psychological health problems can develop. For this reason, it is important that you learn to cope with the stressful events in your life and that you take time to take care of yourself when stress begins to overwhelm you.

F. COMPREHENSION: *ON YOUR OWN*

F.1 True or False

Read each statement about the reading and then circle *True* or *False*. If the statement is false, correct it.

1. Occasional stress is bad for a person's general health.   **True**   **False**

_____

2. There is an exact definition of stress.   **True**   **False**

_____

3. Stress comes from positive and negative situations.   **True**   **False**

_____

4. It is important to be completely stress-free as often as possible.   **True**   **False**

_____

5. Some stress in life is normal.   **True**   **False**

_____

6. All stress is dangerous.   **True**   **False**

_____

7. Our systems for coping with situations in our lives usually work well.   **True**   **False**

_____

8. Chronic stress can lead to serious physical problems.   **True**   **False**

_____

F.2. Completing an Outline

Stress

I. **What is stress?**

     A. _____

_____

B. _____

_____

II. _____

A. Stress is usually a normal part of life.

B. _____

C. Stress does not usually continue for a long time.

D. _____

III. **Chronic stress**

A. _____

B. _____

C. It is important to learn to cope with stress in your life.

TABLE 7.1 Study the patterns for talking about **actions that started in the past and continue now.**

The new students	**have**	**arrived**.
The teacher	**has**	**learned** the students' names.
We	**haven't**	**received** our money.
Have	the new students	(ever) **arrived**?
Has	the teacher	(ever) **learned** the students' names?

TABLE 7.2 Study the patterns for some **irregular verbs.**

Simple Form	Past	Past Participle
be	was / were	been
become	became	become
begin	began	begun
come	came	come
feel	felt	felt
get	got	gotten
go	went	gone
have	had	had
lose	lost	lost
send	sent	sent
sleep	slept	slept
speak	spoke	spoken
take	took	taken
write	wrote	written

G. ORAL PRACTICE: *IN PAIRS*

Use the phrases below to ask questions. Then answer the questions with a short answer. If the answer is affirmative, ask your partner how he or she felt in this situation. Take turns asking and answering. Use *ever* in the question to mean at any time in the past. Follow the model, the patterns in Table 7.1, and the verb forms in Table 7.2.

MODEL: have an operation
      Partner A: *Have you ever had an operation?*
      Partner B: *Yes, I have.*

      Partner A: *How did you feel?*
      Partner B: *I was nervous.*

1. have a flat tire	11. get married
2. become engaged	12. lock your keys in your car
3. travel overseas	13. miss a class
4. argue with your father	14. get a promotion
5. lose your wallet	15. have an accident with your car
6. miss a flight	16. get a traffic ticket
7. speak a foreign language	17. live in a foreign country
8. fail a test	18. live in a big city
9. take a TOEFL exam	19. go to the emergency room
10. study for an important exam	20. work too much

TABLE 7.3   **Study the patterns for using since and for.**

	for	five years. three months. a few weeks. a few minutes.
The students have studied English	**since**	July. last month. Tuesday. 3:30.

H. WRITTEN PRACTICE: *ON YOUR OWN*

Write each sentence below again, using the time expression in parentheses. Use *since* or *for* where necessary. Follow the model and the patterns in Table 7.3.

MODEL: The students waited for the bus. (thirty minutes)

    The students waited for the bus for thirty minutes.

1. I have lived in the United States. (six months)

_____

2. Lisa and Maggie have been upset. (this morning)

_____

3. We lived in New York. (two years)

_____

4. Mike has suffered from the effects of chronic stress. (a long time)

_____

5. The students have been nervous about the exam. (yesterday)

_____

6. The doctor has been with the patient. (2:00)

_____

7. That student has not attended classes. (the beginning of the term)

_____

8. Before her divorce, my sister was married. (five years)

_____

9. I have worked. (ten hours)

_____

10. After the accident, Sam was in the hospital. (a week)

_____

I.   WRITTEN PRACTICE: *ON YOUR OWN*

Look at Table 7.2 on page 182 again.   Then, underline the correct verb tense to complete each sentence below. Follow the model.

MODEL: I (experienced / <u>have experienced</u>) a lot of stress since I left my country.

1. Almost everyone (experienced / has experienced) stress at some time in life.

2. When the teacher (called on / has called on) me yesterday, I felt anxious.

3. After the stressful situation ended, my blood pressure (dropped / has dropped) to normal.

4. Since I (arrived / have arrived) here three weeks ago, I have been a little homesick.

5. Even though I (did not study / have not studied) for my math exam last week, I got a good grade.

6. Tom (suffers / has suffered) from symptoms of chronic stress since 1990.

7. His serious physiological problems (began / have begun) ten years ago.

8. Susan (divorced / has divorced) her husband last year.

9. When a stressful situation (ended / has ended), the heart rate slows down again.

10. Martha (did not cope / has not coped) well with her problems since last summer.

J. ORAL AND WRITTEN PRACTICE: *IN SMALL GROUPS*

Everyone experiences stress, but international students who are living in a foreign country far from home and speaking a foreign language may suffer especially from stress. Look at the case of Miguel below. Discuss this information with your group. Then, using the cue words, write sentences that show completed action in the past or action that started in the past and continues now. Use *for* or *since* where necessary. Check your answers with your classmates. Follow the model.

FIGURE 7.2

Education
- entered the university in 1991; studies marketing
- takes full load of academic courses every term

Family
- older brother came to the United States with him in 1990 and stayed for one month
- mother calls every week; began to call when he arrived
- family sent him a little money from 1991 to present
- father died from heart attack three months ago

Employment
- worked as assistant in his father's company from 1988 to 1989
- works in the university library; began two months after his father died

Health
- not able to sleep well; began to have sleeping problems two weeks ago
- worried about mother
- not hungry; loss of appetite began one week ago

MODEL: Miguel / work / in the library / three months

Miguel has worked in the university library for three months.

1. Miguel / work / in father's office / two years

2. his father / have / heart attack / three months ago

3. Miguel / take / full load of courses / every term / 1991

4. his mother / call / every week / he arrived in the United States

5. Miguel / not eat / much / one week

6. his brother / stay / in United States / one month

7. Miguel / study / marketing / 1991

_____

8. his family / send / him / money / 1991

_____

9. Miguel / not sleep / well / two weeks

_____

10. Miguel / worry / about / his mother / three months

_____

K. WRITTEN PRACTICE: *ON YOUR OWN*

Is your experience in this country similar to Miguel's? Think about your life since you arrived here. Think about your education, family, employment, and health. Fill in the chart below with your ideas. Next, use your ideas to write ten sentences about your life. Be sure that at least five of them are about actions that started in the past and continue now.

CHART 7.2

Education	Family	Employment	Health

1. _____

2. _____

3. _____

4. _____

5. _____

6. _____

7. _____

8. _____

9. _____

10. _____

L. WRITTEN PRACTICE: *ON YOUR OWN*

Use the cues words below to write questions about stress among students. Write about actions that started in the past and continue now.

1. how long / you / be / student / at the university

_____

2. what / be / the most stressful / part / of university life

_____

3. what / help / you / to cope / with stress

_____

4. how often / you / feel / stress / recently

_____

5. what / effects of stress / you / feel

_____

6. when / you / experience / the most stress

_____

7. who / you / talk to / about your feelings

_____

8. where / you / go / to find help / with your personal problems

_____

9. how often / you / go / there

_____

10. how / stress / affect / your work

_____

M. ORAL PRACTICE: *WITH YOUR CLASS*

Form questions from these sentences. Ask about the words in dark print. Follow the model.

MODEL: **Everyone** has experienced stress.
             Who has experienced stress?

1. **Both positive and negative situations** have caused people to feel stress.
2. The students have been worried about **their English test** for several days.
3. Doctors have been aware of the effects of stress **for many years**.
4. Many people have had symptoms of stress **after the death of a family member.**
5. **People with high-stress professions** have more stress than people with low-stress professions.
6. **Stress** has caused serious symptoms for some people.
7. Research about the effects of stress has been done **recently**.
8. Li has felt **anxious** about his future since he became a student.
9. A person may experience more stress **because he or she has not gotten enough sleep.**
10. Most people have suffered **the effects of daily stress.**
11. Students experience stress **when they take exams.**
12. **Lack of sleep** can cause stress.
13. Some people feel **nervous** when they fly.
14. A person's heart rate goes up **when he or she feels stress**.
15. Susan **rarely** feels depressed.
16. Carlos is upset **because he lost his wallet at the bus station.**

N. Taking a Survey: *In Pairs*

Choose five of the questions that you wrote in Exercise L to take a survey. Write the questions on the lines below. Ask five people to answer the questions orally for you. Give each person (subject) a number. Also, write down the person's age and circle *M* (male) or *F* (female) for the person's sex. Finally, write down the person's nationality. After getting all that information, write down each person's answer to your questions. Use a form like the one below to record the responses.

Subject # _____

Age: _____ Sex: M   F   Nationality: _____

1. _____

2. _____

3. _____

4. _____

5. _____

O. Reporting Results: *With Your Class*

With your partner in Exercise N, report the results of your survey to the rest of the class. Record your answers on the board. After all of the groups have reported, compare answers. Discuss the results with your classmates and teacher.

P. Writing a Summary: *On Your Own*

Using the information from your survey and ideas you got from discussing the results with the class, write a paragraph about stress among the people you surveyed. Include information from your survey. You may use any verb tense that you think will work well. In choosing the verb tense for each sentence, consider the following: Did the action begin in the past and is it continuing now? Is the action occurring now, or is the action habitual? Did the action begin in the past and finish in the past?

Most people have experienced stress. _____

_____

_____

_____

_____

_____

_____

_____

_____

The Effects of Stress

LESSON 2

FIGURE 7.3

A. WARM-UP: *IN SMALL GROUPS*

Look at the pictures above. What can you guess about the lifestyles of these people? Do you think their lifestyles are different? Why or why not? With your group, make a list of your ideas. Discuss these ideas with your class.

B. DISCUSSION: *WITH YOUR CLASS*

Try to answer these questions in a class discussion.

1. What do you think are some of the physical problems that stress might cause?
2. What might be some of the psychological problems?
3. Which person in the pictures do you think has better health? Why?
4. Do you think that any of the people in the pictures above could change his or her behavior for better health?

C. FOCUS VOCABULARY: *ON YOUR OWN*

On the lines below, write the new words that you learn in class. Add to your list as you study the effects of stress. Focus on new nouns and adjectives.

_____   _____   _____

_____   _____   _____

_____   _____   _____

_____   _____   _____

_____   _____   _____

D. LISTENING PRACTICE: *ON YOUR OWN*

Listen as your teacher tells you about the effects of stress. Write down important information about this in the chart below. After listening, compare your chart with those of your classmates.

CHART 7.3

THE EFFECTS OF STRESS	
Short-term	
Physical Effects	Psychological Effects
Long-term	
Physical Effects	Psychological Effects

E.   COMPREHENSION: *ON YOUR OWN*

E.1. True or False

Read each of these statements and circle *True* or *False*. If the statement is false, correct it.

1. A person who has just experienced stress has a slow heartbeat.   **True**   **False**

_____

2. The body needs to rest between stressful situations.   **True**   **False**

_____

3. Depression is a long-term physiological effect.   **True**   **False**

_____

4. Fear is an emotional response to stress.   **True**   **False**

_____

5. Normal stress is not dangerous.   **True**   **False**

_____

6. Stress can affect concentration.   **True**   **False**

_____

7. Heart disease can be an effect of continued stress.   **True**   **False**

_____

8. Usually, the blood pressure drops when a stressful situation has ended.   **True**   **False**

_____

9. Confusion is a psychological effect of stress.   **True**   **False**

_____

10. Dry mouth is a physical effect of stress.   **True**   **False**

_____

E.2. Comprehension Questions

Using information from Chart 7.3 on page 190, answer the following questions about the effects of stress.

1. What are three common short-term effects of stress?

_____

2. When do the short-term effects of occasional stress end?

_____

3. What can happen to blood pressure if stress continues for a long period of time?

_____

4. What are two short-term psychological effects of stress?

_____

5. What is one severe long-term psychological effect of stress?

_____

6. When can stress become a problem?

_____

F. WRITING A SUMMARY: *ON YOUR OWN*

Use the information in Chart 7.3 to write a short summary of the short-term effects of stress.

_____

_____

_____

_____

_____

G. ORAL PRACTICE: *IN PAIRS*

Using the cue words below, take turns asking and answering questions. Decide if the action was completed in the past or if the action started in the past and continues now. Use short answers. Follow the model.

MODEL: you / feel / nervous / recently
                  Partner A: *Have you felt nervous recently?*
                  Partner B: *No, I haven't.*

1. you / finish / your assignment / last night
2. you / find / a good place to live / yet
3. you / study English / before / you arrived
4. the language / be / difficult / for you / at first
5. you / get / any exercise / since you arrived here
6. your parents / go / to the airport / with you / when you left home
7. you / find / cultural difference / when / you arrived here
8. you / improve / your English skills / since / you arrived
9. the weather / here / surprise / you
10. the food / here / make / you / sick / at first
11. you / have / any trouble / since you arrived here
12. you / call / your family / last weekend

H. CASE STUDIES: *IN SMALL GROUPS*

Read the information in the cases below. Each of these people is a patient at General Hospital. Each one has a different problem. Imagine that your group is a team of doctors which will be treating and advising each of the patients about his or her health condition. You have already prescribed the appropriate medicine for each patient. Now you must give advice about how each can improve his or her health.

Look at each patient's medical record and discuss it. Then, make a list of the things each patient should and shouldn't do. After each group has finished, meet with the whole class to compare advice. Discuss your suggestions with the class.

Case #1
MEDICAL RECORD

Patient's name __John Martin__ Age __45__ Marital Status __divorced__ Children __two__

Ages of children __20, 18__ Occupation __truck driver__

Height __5'8"__ Weight __250 lbs.__ Exercise __none__

Does the patient smoke? __yes__ Does the patient drink? __yes__

Symptoms __chest pains; very high blood pressure__

Comments __needs exercise; must stop smoking; needs to lose weight__

Case #2
MEDICAL RECORD

Patient's name __Lisa Johnson__ Age __30__ Marital Status __married__ Children __none__

Ages of children _____ Occupation __bank president__

Height __5'6"__ Weight __135 lbs.__ Exercise __jogs 5 times a week__

Does the patient smoke? __no__ Does the patient drink? __no__

Symptoms __High blood pressure; headaches__

Comments __needs to stop using salt on food; needs a vacation__

Case #3
MEDICAL RECORD

Patient's name __Margaret White__ Age __40__ Marital Status __married__ Children __5__

Ages of children __1–6__ Occupation __mother, housewife__

Height __5'5"__ Weight __200 lbs.__ Exercise __plays tennis once a week__

Does the patient smoke? __no__ Does the patient drink? __no__

Symptoms __Always tired; losing memory; rapid heart beat__

Comments __needs a vacation; needs to lose weight__

I. ORAL PRACTICE: *WITH YOUR CLASS*

Use the information in the medical records above to answer these questions with a short answer. Follow the model.

MODEL: Who is the youngest patient?
Lisa Johnson is.

1. Who is the oldest patient?
2. Who has the most stressful occupation?
3. Which patient smokes cigarettes?
4. Which one gets the least exercise?
5. Who is the heaviest patient?
6. Which patient has the worst symptoms?
7. Who has the youngest children?
8. Which one has the most stressful life?
9. Who needs the longest vacation?
10. Who has the least stressful occupation?
11. Which one has the highest blood pressure?
12. Who has no children?

TABLE 7.4   **Study the patterns for using should to give advice.**

The patients	**should**	**get** more exercise.
Some of them	**should**	**change** their jobs.
They	**shouldn't**	**smoke** cigarettes.
Should	people	**eat** less fat?

J. WRITTEN PRACTICE: *ON YOUR OWN*

Look at the information given about each patient in Exercise H on page 193. Write five sentences using *should* or *shouldn't* for each of the three patients. Follow the model and the patterns in Table 7.4.

MODEL:

Mrs. White should lose about twenty pounds.

Case #1

1. _____
2. _____
3. _____
4. _____
5. _____

Case #2

1. _____
2. _____
3. _____
4. _____
5. _____

Case #3

1. _____

2. _____

3. _____

4. _____

5. _____

K.   DISCUSSION: *WITH YOUR CLASS*

Use the information in the medical records and the sentences that you wrote in Exercise J to discuss the advice that each patient should follow. Compare your suggestions with those of your classmates. Do you agree with your classmates' advice?

Managing Stress
LESSON 3

FIGURE 7.4

(LEFT) © ELIZABETH CREWS/THE IMAGE WORKS; (RIGHT) ADAM TANNER © 1989/COMSTOCK; (BOTTOM) BONNIE KAMIN © 1989/ COMSTOCK

A.   WARM-UP: *WITH YOUR CLASS*

Look at the pictures above. What are the people doing? Do you think that these activities help people to reduce stress? What do you do to manage stress? Together with your classmates, make a list of things that people can do to help manage stress. Talk about each item on the list. How does it help to reduce stress?

B.   COMPLETING A QUESTIONNAIRE: *ON YOUR OWN*

The following test was developed by the psychologists Lyle H. Miller and Alma Dell Smith at Boston University Medical Center. Score each item from 1 (almost always) to 5 (never), according to how much of the time each statement applies to you.

HOW VULNERABLE ARE YOU TO STRESS?

_____ 1. I EAT AT LEAST ONE HOT, BALANCED MEAL A DAY.

_____ 2. I GET SEVEN TO EIGHT HOURS OF SLEEP AT LEAST FOUR NIGHTS A WEEK.

_____ 3. I GIVE AND RECEIVE AFFECTION FROM MY FAMILY AND FRIENDS.

_____ 4. I HAVE AT LEAST ONE RELATIVE WITHIN FIFTY MILES WHO WILL ALWAYS HELP ME.

_____ 5. I EXERCISE VIGOROUSLY AT LEAST TWICE A WEEK.

_____ 6. I SMOKE LESS THAN HALF A PACK OF CIGARETTES A DAY.

_____ 7. I TAKE FEWER THAN FIVE ALCOHOLIC DRINKS A WEEK.

_____ 8. I DO NOT WEIGH TOO MUCH OR TOO LITTLE FOR MY HEIGHT.

_____ 9. I HAVE ENOUGH MONEY TO MEET MY BASIC EXPENSES.

_____ 10. I GET STRENGTH FROM MY RELIGIOUS BELIEFS.

_____ 11. I REGULARLY ATTEND CLUB OR SOCIAL ACTIVITIES.

_____ 12. I HAVE SEVERAL CLOSE FRIENDS AND MANY ACQUAINTANCES.

_____ 13. I HAVE ONE OR MORE FRIENDS THAT I CAN TELL MY PERSONAL PROBLEMS TO.

_____ 14. I AM IN GOOD HEALTH (INCLUDING EYESIGHT, HEARING, AND TEETH).

_____ 15. I AM ABLE TO TALK OPENLY ABOUT MY FEELINGS WHEN I AM ANGRY OR WORRIED.

_____ 16. I CAN TALK TO THE PEOPLE THAT I LIVE WITH ABOUT DOMESTIC PROBLEMS (HOUSEWORK, MONEY, ETC.)

_____ 17. I DO SOMETHING FOR FUN AT LEAST ONCE A WEEK.

_____ 18. I AM ABLE TO ORGANIZE MY TIME WELL.

_____ 19. I DRINK FEWER THAN THREE CUPS OF COFFEE, TEA, OR COLA DRINKS A DAY.

_____ 20. I TAKE QUIET TIME FOR MYSELF DURING THE DAY.

_____ TOTAL

To get your score, add up the figures and subtract 20. Any number over 30 means that you are vulnerable to stress. You are seriously vulnerable to stress if your score is between 50 and 75 and extremely vulnerable if it is over 75.

C. FOCUS VOCABULARY: *ON YOUR OWN*

On the lines below, write down any new words that you learn in class. Add to your list as you study about managing stress. Focus on adjectives and nouns.

_____   _____   _____

_____   _____   _____

_____   _____   _____

TABLE 7.5   Study the patterns using **could** to talk about possibility.

| I | **could** | **study** | tonight | or | I | **could** **go** to a movie with a friend. |
| We | **could** | **eat** | at home | or | we | **could** **eat** in a restaurant. |

D. WRITTEN PRACTICE: *IN PAIRS*

Now, share your answers to the questionnaire on page 196 with a partner. Look at the answers and give advice about things that he or she could do to reduce vulnerability to stress. Then, write eight sentences about changes that your partner could make in his or her life. Follow the model and the patterns in Table 7.5.

MODEL: *Marco could get more sleep.*

Amina could talk to her friends about her feelings.

1. _____

2. _____

3. _____

4. _____

5. _____

6. _____

7. _____

8. _____

E.   READING   *Managing Stress*

All people manage the stress in their lives in one way or another. Some are successful managers of stress and some are not. Managing stress is a skill that can be learned in the same way that one learns to manage money or to manage time. Different people find different methods of managing stress. Even though everyone manages stress in his or her own way, there are some common factors. Here are ten suggestions for helping people manage stress.

1. Get organized. Disorganization can cause stress. Having too many things to do or places to be at the same time can lead to confusion, forgetfulness, and worry about getting everything done on time. Try to do one thing at a time. Give yourself time to relax between projects.
2. Have reasonable goals. Most people set goals that are unreasonable and impossible to reach. No one is perfect, and everyone fails to reach some goals. Set goals that you can reach.
3. Learn to enjoy yourself. People need to get away from the pressure and problems of life and have fun. Take short vacations occasionally. Find hobbies that take your attention and are enjoyable.
4. Think positively. Avoid criticizing others. Look for good characteristics in yourself and in other people.
5. Be tolerant and forgiving. Being intolerant of others can cause frustration and anger. Try to accept people the way they are. Don't try to change them.
6. Avoid competition. There are some competitive situations in life that we cannot avoid. But too much worrying about winning can lead to anxiety and tension. It can also make us aggressive.
7. Get regular physical exercise. Exercise helps to reduce the physical effects of stress. Choose an activity that you enjoy so that you will continue to do it regularly.
8. Learn a drug-free way to relax. Try meditation, yoga, massage, warm baths, or other natural methods of relaxation.
9. Talk about your problems. Talk with a friend, a therapist, or a counselor. Expressing your emotions can be very helpful in reducing stress.
10. Know yourself. Be aware of the amount of stress that you are comfortable with. Know when it is time to step back and take a break.

F.   ANSWERING SHORT ESSAY QUESTIONS: *ON YOUR OWN*

Answer the following questions using the information from the reading above and your own ideas. Answer each question with three to five sentences. Use your own words.

1. Why should a person exercise? How can regular exercise help to reduce stress?

_____

_____

_____

_____

2. Why should a person be organized? How can being organized help a person to reduce stress?

_____

_____

_____

_____

3. Why shouldn't a person use drugs or alcohol to relax?

_____

_____

_____

_____

G.   ORAL PRACTICE: *IN PAIRS*

Using the information in the reading above and your own knowledge, take turns asking and answering questions. Use the cue words and follow the model.

MODEL: be organized
        Partner A: *Why should people be organized?*
        Partner B: *People should be organized because life is easier when you are organized.*

1. set reasonable goals
2. have time to relax
3. take vacations
4. avoid competition
5. try meditation
6. exercise
7. be forgiving
8. talk about problems
9. have fun
10. learn natural ways to relax
11. avoid criticizing others
12. express emotions

H.   WRITTEN PRACTICE: *ON YOUR OWN*

Answer the following questions, using *could*. Follow the model.

MODEL: How could a disorganized person reduce stress?

      He or she could get organized.

1. How could a person who hates his job reduce stress?

_____

2. How could an angry person reduce stress?

_____

3. How could a negative person reduce stress?

_____

4. How could a tense person relax?

_____

5. How could a person learn to relax?

_____

6. How could a competitive person reduce stress?

_____

7. How could a person who works in an office all day reduce stress?

_____

8. How could a person who has a very difficult job reduce stress?

_____

I. WRITTEN PRACTICE: *ON YOUR OWN*

Review the patterns for *can, could, must,* and *should.* Think about their meanings. Use them to fill in the blanks below.

1. Mrs. Jones needs to buy new glasses and she wants to buy a new television. She doesn't have

   enough money for both the glasses and the television. If she buys the television, she

   _____ use her old glasses. If she does this, it _____ cause a

   dangerous situation when she drives. I think that she _____ buy the glasses now

   and wait to buy the television.

2. The employees at the Ace Hightop Shoe Company _____ arrive for work by

   8:00 A.M. If workers are going to be late, they _____ call the office to let the

   manager know when they will arrive.

3. People who are very tense _____ learn to manage their stress. They

   _____ talk to someone about their problems.

4. When people are competitive, they _____ relax and enjoy their work. In fact, if

   they don't learn to manage their stress, they _____ develop a stress-related illness.

5. Mr. Smith is upset because he _____ pay so much money for taxes. He feels angry

because the government spends part of the money on nuclear power plants. He doesn't think that

he _____ pay taxes for nuclear power. He doesn't like this situation, but what

_____ he do?

J. KEEPING A JOURNAL: *ON YOUR OWN*

For one day, keep a journal of things in your life that cause you to feel stress. Write down each stressful event and how it made you feel. At the end of the day, take a few minutes to think about how you managed each stressful situation and how you might manage stress in the future.

K. WRITING A SUMMARY: *ON YOUR OWN*

Look at the journal that you kept for Exercise J. Using the information in your journal and information that you have learned from this chapter, write a paragraph about the things that can cause you stress and how you could manage this stress.

_____

_____

_____

_____

_____

_____

_____

_____

_____

_____

_____

_____

_____

_____

_____

_____

_____

FIGURE 8.1   Advertising

Now part of the pleasure of a hot bowl of soup can be feeling good about what you're not eating.

With Campbell's® Special Request,® you can choose from eight delicious soups that understand what you want and what you don't want.

Each has 1/3 less salt than our regular soups. Every one is low in cholesterol. Every one has less than 150 calories; most have less than 100.

And the good news gets better with every sip. You'll taste the rich broth, all the satisfying meat, vegetables or pasta—the special warmth that comes with a great bowl of soup.

M'm! M'm! Good!®

A soup you can count on.

© 1990 Campbell Soup Company

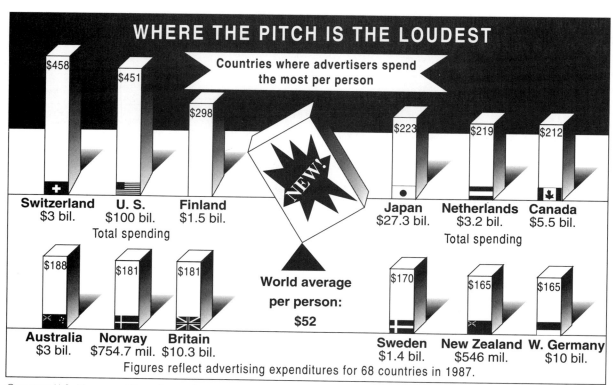

WHERE THE PITCH IS THE LOUDEST

Countries where advertisers spend the most per person

$458 — **Switzerland** $3 bil.
$451 — **U. S.** $100 bil. Total spending
$298 — **Finland** $1.5 bil.

NEW!

$223 — **Japan** $27.3 bil.
$219 — **Netherlands** $3.2 bil. Total spending
$212 — **Canada** $5.5 bil.

$188 — **Australia** $3 bil.
$181 — **Norway** $754.7 mil.
$181 — **Britain** $10.3 bil.

World average per person: $52

$170 — **Sweden** $1.4 bil.
$165 — **New Zealand** $546 mil.
$165 — **W. Germany** $10 bil.

Figures reflect advertising expenditures for 68 countries in 1987.

Advertising
CHAPTER 8

Advertising in American Society
LESSON 1

A. WARM-UP: *WITH YOUR CLASS*

Think about the advertisements that you have seen on TV or in magazines since you arrived in this country. Are they different from or similar to ads shown in your country? Discuss your ideas with your teacher. Try to answer the following questions as you talk.

1. Are there more or fewer ads on TV here than in your country?
2. Are ads shown at the same time as ads in your country?
3. Do ads in this country try to sell products that are different from the products they try to sell in your country?
4. Are the styles of the ads similar or different?
5. What is the biggest difference between advertising here and in your country?
6. What is the most surprising advertisement you have seen on TV or in a magazine?
7. What is the best advertisement you have seen so far?
8. What is the worst advertisement you have seen?

B. DISCUSSION: *IN SMALL GROUPS*

Look at the advertisements in Figure 8.1. With your group, answer these questions and then share your answers with your classmates.

1. What products are these ads trying to sell? How can you tell?
2. What promises do the ads make about the products?
3. Why would people want to buy these products?
4. What are the advertisers trying to make you believe about their products?
5. How will your life change if you buy these products, according to the ads?
6. Do you like these ads? Do they make you want to buy the product? Why or why not?

C. FOCUS VOCABULARY: *ON YOUR OWN*

On the lines below, write down any new words that you learn in class. Add to your list as you study about advertising in American society. Focus on new adjectives and adverbs.

_____ _____ _____

_____ _____ _____

_____ _____ _____

_____ _____ _____

D. READING   *The Business of Advertising*

Advertising is a Business

Advertising can be seen everywhere in American society. We find advertisements on television, in movies, on the radio, on billboards by the highway, on buses, on benches, in magazines, in the mail, in stores, and even on our clothing. It is nearly impossible to escape from advertising.

Advertising is big business. It plays a large and important role in the economy of the United States. In 1987, approximately $100 billion was spent on advertising. That equals about $451 per man, woman, and child in the country. Thousands of different types of businesses, institutions, and individuals use advertising to help them sell their products and services. In addition, service organizations, special-interest groups, and even political candidates advertise.

Importance of Advertising to Our Lifestyle and the Economy

Why is advertising so important? Without ads we could not live the way we do today. In the United States and other parts of the world, men and women use hundreds of consumer products every day. Things that people thought of as luxuries in the past, such as shampoo, felt-tipped pens, and televisions are now necessary parts of our lives. Because of our ability to mass produce goods at relatively low prices, advertising is a way to let people know about products.

Without advertising the economy would suffer. Large quantities of goods would be produced, but few people would know about them and even fewer would want to buy them. Soon unsold goods would fill warehouses, production would stop, and factories would shut down. If the factories closed, thousands of people would lose their jobs. They wouldn't be able to afford even basic consumer goods. This would not be good for the country's economy.

E.   COMPREHENSION: *ON YOUR OWN*

E.1. True or False

Read each statement about the reading and then circle *True* or *False*. If the statement is false, correct it.

1. Advertising has very little effect on the economy.   **True**   **False**

2. Shampoo is a luxury for most people today.   **True**   **False**

3. Mass production provides large numbers of consumer goods.   **True**   **False**

4. In 1987, American advertisers spent more than $1,000 on each person in the United States.   **True**   **False**

5. Only businesses advertise.   **True**   **False**

6. If manufacturers and businesses did not advertise, many people would be out of work. **True**   **False**

7. Without advertising, consumers would not know about the goods that are available. **True**   **False**

8. Life would be the same with or without advertising. **True**   **False**

9. People don't believe that televisions are necessary for daily living. **True**   **False**

10. Advertising in the United States is limited to newspaper, radio, and television. **True**   **False**

E.2. Outlining

Complete the outline below, using information from the reading.

Advertising in American Society

I. **Advertising is a business.**

    A. _____

        1. _____

        2. at the movies

        3. _____

        4. _____

        5. _____

        6. on benches

        7. _____

        8. _____

        9. _____

        10. on clothing

    B. It is big business.

        1. _____

        2. Businesses, institutions, and individuals advertise.

        3. _____

II. **Advertising is important to the economy.**

    A.   Without ads we couldn't live the way we do.

        1. _____

        2. Advertising lets people know about products.

    B. _____

        1. Few people would buy.

        2. _____

        3. Production would stop.

        4. _____

        5. People would lose their jobs.

        6. _____

TABLE 8.1   **Study the patterns for talking about unreal conditions.**

If companies **didn't sell** products, If companies **produced** fewer products	they	**wouldn't** **make** money. **would** **lose** money. **wouldn't** **be** in business.
OR		

Companies   **wouldn't make** money
            would lose money
            wouldn't be in business
	if they	**produced** fewer products.
		didn't make money.

Would companies **make** money	if they	**produced** fewer products?
OR		
If companies **produced** fewer products, What **would happen**		**would** they **make** money? if companies **produced** fewer products?
OR		
If companies **produced** fewer products,		what **would happen**?

F. ORAL PRACTICE: *WITH YOUR CLASS*

Your teacher will ask you some questions about advertising. Use information in the reading on page 204 and your own ideas to answer the questions. Follow the patterns in Table 8.1.

1. What would happen if factories stopped producing consumer goods?
2. What would you buy if you had a million dollars?
3. What would happen if a business didn't advertise its products?

4. How much would you spend if you needed a new car?
5. What would happen if people didn't buy mass-produced goods?
6. What would happen if political candidates didn't advertise?
7. What would happen if businesses didn't advertise on TV?
8. What would happen if people stopped spending money on cars?

G. WRITTEN PRACTICE: *ON YOUR OWN*

Use the word cues below to write sentences about unreal situations. Follow the model and the patterns in Table 8.1.

MODEL: if manufactures / advertise (negative) / they sell (negative) / their products

If manufactures didn't advertise, they wouldn't sell their products.

1. if people / know (negative) / about products / they buy (negative) / them

_____

2. if people / stop buying / products / factories / close

_____

3. if workers / lose / their jobs / they / buy (negative) / many consumer goods

_____

4. if advertisers / put (negative) / ads on TV / no one / know / about their products

_____

5. if consumers / listen (negative) to ads / they know (negative) / what to buy

_____

6. if factories / close down / workers / lose / their jobs

_____

7. if consumers / spend (negative) / money / the economy / suffer

_____

8. if companies / buy (negative) / advertising / consumers / know (negative) / their choices

_____

9. if newspapers / carry (negative) advertisements / they / go / out of business

_____

10. if advertisers / put (negative) / ads / on billboards / drivers / see (negative) the ads

_____

H. ORAL PRACTICE: *IN PAIRS*

Take turns asking and answering questions about unreal situations. Follow the model.

MODEL: shop at Wilsons
           Partner A: *Why would you shop at Wilsons?*
           Partner B: *I would shop at Wilsons if I needed new tires.*

1. buy skis
2. sell your car
3. put an ad in the newspaper
4. put your money in the bank
5. buy a new bicycle

6. buy insurance
7. get a new car
8. move to a new apartment
9. begin an exercise program
10. take a TOEFL exam

11. play the lottery
12. change classes
13. go to a movie
14. go to another school

I. WRITTEN PRACTICE: *ON YOUR OWN*

Write a statement about each unreal situation described below. Begin each statement with *I would / wouldn't buy it / them if...*

MODEL: This car is very small. I have a large family.

I would buy it if I had a small family.

1. These tickets are for an eight o'clock movie. I work until eight-thirty.

_____

2. This dinner comes with pasta. I don't like pasta.

_____

3. This car gets only fifteen miles per gallon of gas. I want to save gas.

_____

4. This cassette is thirty minutes long. My class is forty-five minutes long.

_____

5. These eggs aren't fresh. I want to make a cake now.

_____

6. This apartment has one bedroom. I have three children.

_____

7. This book is about home finance. I want a book about home repair.

_____

8. This shampoo is for oily hair. I have dry hair.

_____

9. This ring is silver. I want a gold ring.

_____

10. That house isn't finished yet. I want to buy a house now.

_____

11. These bananas are not ripe. I need to use them today.

_____

12. That stereo doesn't have a CD player. I have a large CD collection.

_____

13. These shoes are size six. I wear a size nine.

_____

14. This candy has a lot of sugar. I am on a diet.

_____

J. WRITTEN PRACTICE: *ON YOUR OWN*

When advertisers want to sell a new product, they ask some consumers for their opinions. They want to know why a consumer would buy the product. Below is a description of a new shampoo. Read the description and then, using the phrases given, write sentences about why you would or wouldn't buy this shampoo. Follow the model.

Our new shampoo contains no harsh chemicals. It has only natural ingredients. It will not make your hair dry or difficult to manage. It will clean you hair gently. This shampoo will make your hair shine. Your hair will smell clean and fresh. Your hair will be soft and healthy. Our shampoo will make you very attractive. Our shampoo is not very expensive.

MODEL: clean

   I wouldn't buy this shampoo if it didn't clean well.

          OR

   I would buy this shampoo if it cleaned well.

1. natural ingredients

_____

2. gently

_____

3. shine

_____

4. difficult to manage

_____

5. harsh chemicals

_____

6. attractive

_____

7. healthy

_____

8. expensive

_____

K. GIVING A PRESENTATION: *WITH YOUR CLASS*

Tear an advertisement from a newspaper or magazine. Look at it carefully and make a list of the positive and negative aspects of the product advertised. For example, if you are looking at an ad for a used car, think about the car's price, age, condition, and special features such as air conditioning, gas mileage, power windows, automatic transmission, and so forth. Use your list to give a short presentation about why you would or wouldn't want to buy the product.

L. WRITING A SUMMARY: *ON YOUR OWN*

Write a summary about why you would or wouldn't buy the product you described in Exercise K.

_____

_____

_____

_____

_____

_____

_____

_____

Types of Advertising
LESSON 2

FIGURE 8.2

A. WARM UP: *WITH YOUR CLASS*

On the board, make a list of different places where you can see and hear advertising. Try to group the items in your list according to the type of media used for advertising. Use the headings on the chart below to help you classify the items on the list.

CHART 8.1

Print	Broadcast	Outdoor	Direct Mail

B. DISCUSSION: *WITH YOUR CLASS*

For the next twenty-four hours, pay attention to the number of advertisements you see and hear. Note the types of ads you see. Discuss the ads that you've seen with your class.

C. ORAL PRACTICE: *WITH YOUR CLASS*

Answer these questions about products affirmatively, giving a reason for your answer. Follow the model.

MODEL: Will you buy a new coat this winter?
         I will buy a new coat if my old one doesn't fit me.

1. Will you take your car back to the dealer?
2. Will you go shopping this weekend?
3. Will you buy a ticket for the ballet?
4. Will you take a vacation in the summer?
5. Will you try that new restaurant?
6. Will you call me later?
7. Will you buy new books for your classes next term?
8. Will you have dinner with me next Friday?
9. Will you pay your tuition tomorrow?
10. Will you purchase a parking sticker for your car?
11. Will you buy lunch at the student union?
12. Will you send a letter to your family this week?

D. FOCUS VOCABULARY: *ON YOUR OWN*

On the lines below, write down any new words that you learn in class. Add to your list as you study about types of advertising. Focus on new nouns and verbs.

_____   _____   _____

_____   _____   _____

_____   _____   _____

_____   _____   _____

E. LISTENING PRACTICE: *ON YOUR OWN*

Listen as your teacher tells you about different types of advertising. Listen for the information you need to complete the chart below. Then, compare your chart to those of your classmates.

CHART 8.2

Type of Advertising	Advantages	Disadvantages	Interesting Facts

F. COMPREHENSION: *ON YOUR OWN*

F.1. True or False

Read each statement about the passage you heard and then circle *True* or *False*. If the statement is false, correct it.

1. Print advertising is the most expensive form of advertising. **True** **False**

2. Outdoor advertising is more expensive than direct-mail advertising. **True** **False**

3. Radio was the first form of broadcast advertising. **True** **False**

4. Only local businesses advertise in newspapers. **True** **False**

5. Magazines are not usually specialized. **True** **False**

6. Billboards are a form of direct mail. **True** **False**

7. Direct-mail advertising is very effective. **True** **False**

8. People complain that billboards are ugly. **True** **False**

9. Advertisements in magazines cost more than those in newspapers. **True** **False**

10. The messages on billboards are very short. **True** **False**

F.2. Comprehension Questions

Use the information in Chart 8.2 to answer the following questions. Write a complete sentence for each.

1. Why do advertisers prefer to advertise in specialized magazines?

_____

2. Why is direct mail an easy way to advertise?

_____

3. Why do people complain about billboards?

_____

4. Why can television ads be more creative than radio ads?

_____

5. What are two forms of print advertising?

_____

6. What is the cheapest form of advertising?

_____

7. What are two advantages to advertising in newspapers?

_____

TABLE 8.2   Study the patterns for talking about **real conditions**.

If a company	**doesn't advertise,** **fails to advertise,** **advertises too little,**	it	**won't** **will**	**sell** many products. **lose** a lot of money.
	OR			
A company	**won't sell** many products **will lose** a lot of money	if	it **doesn't advertise**. it **advertises** too little.
Will a company **lose** money			if it **doesn't advertise**?	
	OR			
If a company **doesn't advertise**			**will** it **lose** money?	
What **will happen**			if a company **doesn't advertise**?	
	OR			
If a company **doesn't advertise**,			what **will happen**?	

G.   WRITTEN PRACTICE: *ON YOUR OWN*

Use the cue words below to write real sentences about real situations. Follow the model and the patterns in Table 8.2.

MODEL: business / spend (negative) / enough money on advertising / they / sell (negative) / their products

If businesses don't spend enough money on advertising, they won't sell their products.

1. a company / advertise / in the right places / people / buy / its products

_____

2. a small business / have (negative) / much money for advertising / it / advertise / newspapers

_____

3. a company / want to use / sound and action / to advertise a product / it / advertise on TV

_____

4. many people / see / an ad / it / be effective

_____

5. a business / decide / to advertise on TV / it / pay / more for ads

_____

6. your name / be / on a mailing list / businesses / send / you direct / mail ads

_____

7. messages / on a billboard / be / short / drivers / be able to read / them / quickly

_____

8. ads / be (negative) / interesting and entertaining / consumers / pay (negative) attention

_____

9. an ad / be / in color / it / cost / more

_____

10. a company / sell (negative) / sports equipment / it / advertise (negative) / in a sports magazine

_____

H. WRITTEN PRACTICE: *ON YOUR OWN*

Complete the statements below about real situations. Use information from Chart 8.2 on page 212 and your own knowledge. Follow the model.

MODEL: A company will advertise its product on television or radio if *it wants to have*

creative and interesting ads.

1. Local businesses will put their ads in a local newspaper if _____

_____

2. A company will decide to advertise on television if _____

_____

3. Fast food restaurants will put ads on billboards if _____

_____

4. An airline will advertise its low prices in a newspaper instead of on TV if _____

_____

5. A children's toy company will advertise during children's TV programs if _____

_____

6. An advertiser will use direct mail to advertise a product if _____

_____

7. A small company will choose to advertise on the radio rather than on TV if _____

_____

8. A farm-equipment company will advertise in an agriculture magazine if _____

_____

9. A company will choose to advertise in a magazine instead of a newspaper if _____

_____

10. A grocery store will put an ad in the newspaper if _____

_____

11. A small bakery will put an ad on the radio if _____

_____

12. Companies spend a lot of money on their ads if _____

_____

TABLE 8.3   Study the patterns for the **superlative form of adjectives**.

That company has	**the funniest ads**	on TV.
This product has	**the highest price**	of the four products.
Television ads are	**the most expensive**	of all ads.
These ads are	**the most interesting**	of all.
This is	**the best ad**	on TV.
This is	**the worst program**	I have ever seen.

TABLE 8.4   Study the patterns for the **superlative form of nouns**.

This product contains	**the fewest**	vitamins.
	the least	protein.
	the most	sugar.

I. ORAL PRACTICE: *WITH YOUR CLASS*

Look at the three ads on the next page. Discuss the products being sold and answer these questions. Follow the patterns in Tables 8.3 and 8.4.

1. Which cereal has the largest amount of iron?
2. Which one has the least amount of sodium?
3. Which one is the most expensive cereal?
4. Which company has the best ad?
5. Which one is the most nutritious cereal?
6. Which one is the sweetest cereal?
7. Which one has the most interesting ad?
8. Which cereal is the lowest in calories?
9. Which one has the most healthful ingredients?
10. Which one is the most appealing product?

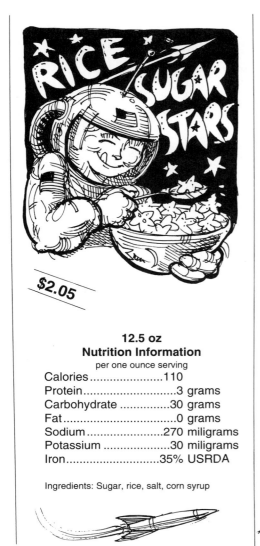

12.5 oz
Nutrition Information
per one ounce serving
Calories......................110
Protein...........................3 grams
Carbohydrate ....30 grams
Fat.................................0 grams
Sodium......................270 miligrams
Potassium ....30 miligrams
Iron...........................35% USRDA

Ingredients: Sugar, rice, salt, corn syrup

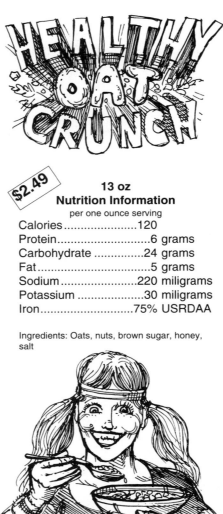

$2.49

13 oz
Nutrition Information
per one ounce serving
Calories......................120
Protein...........................6 grams
Carbohydrate ....24 grams
Fat.................................5 grams
Sodium......................220 miligrams
Potassium ....30 miligrams
Iron...........................75% USRDAA

Ingredients: Oats, nuts, brown sugar, honey, salt

11 oz
Nutrition Information
per one ounce serving
Calories......................125
Protein...........................1 gram
Carbohydrate ....35 grams
Fat.................................4 grams
Sodium......................250 miligrams
Potassium ....30 miligrams
Iron...........................50% USRDA

Ingredients: Sugar, honey, flour, corn syrup, salt

$1.95

FIGURE 8.3

J. WRITTEN PRACTICE: ON YOUR OWN

Fill in each blank with the superlative form of each adjective below. Follow the patterns in Tables 8.3 and 8.4.

1. Laws against false advertising are effective against even _____ ads.
   (dishonest)

2. All of these ads are informative, but this one is _____.
   (informative)

3. The _____ ads on TV are _____.
   (long)   (expensive)

4. _____ advertisements are usually very creative.
   (good)

5. This is one of _____ ads I've ever seen.
   (bad)

6. This ad claims that this car is _____ of all cars to drive.
   (exciting)

7. The news on Channel 7 has some of _____ ads on television.
   (short)

8. A restaurant will advertise that its food is _____ and that its service is
   (delicious)
   _____ in town.
   (quick)

9. Put your money in our bank. We pay _____ rate of interest of all
   banks in this area.   (high)

10. This company offers its services for _____ price in this city.
    (low)

K. READING CHARTS: *ON YOUR OWN*

Look at the charts in Figure 8.4. Discuss them with your class and then write answers to these questions.

1. Which company spent the most money on television advertising in 1987?

_____

2. Which newspaper carried the most advertising in 1989?

_____

3. What type of business had the highest increase in magazine advertising in 1988?

_____

4. What types of companies spent the most on TV ads in 1987? Do you recognize any of the names? What products do they sell?

_____

5. Which of the businesses had the smallest increase in magazine advertising in 1988?

_____

6. Which of the newspapers had the fewest ads in 1989?

_____

7. Which business spent the least on television ads in 1987?

_____

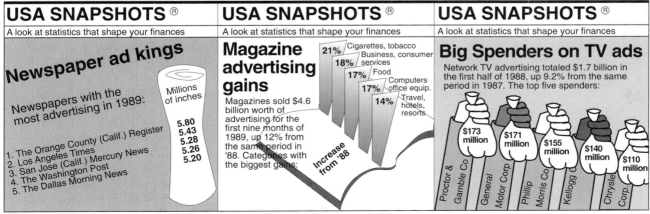

FIGURE 8.4   INFORMATION ADAPTED FROM COPYRIGHTED MATERIAL © 1988, 1989, 1990 USA TODAY WITH PERMISSION.

Truth in Advertising

LESSON 3

The Readiest Road to Health
is by means of PHYSICAL EXERCISE,
and the easiest mode of exercise is by using

VIGOR'S HORSE ACTION SADDLE

as personally orderd by H.R.H. The Princess of Monaco
Which not only provides, as Dr. George Fleming writes:
"A PERFECT SUBSTITUTE FOR THE LIVE HORSE," but acts so
beneficially upon the system as to be of priceless value. It
- •PROMOTES GOOD SPIRITS
  - •QUICKENS THE CIRCULATION
    - •STIMULATES THE LIVER
  - •REDUCES CORPULENCE
    - •CREATES APPETITE and
      - •AIDS DIGESTION
Makes Life Brighter and Happier.
Particulars, with ILLUSTRATIONS, Poast Free. Side Saddles for Ladies.

FIGURE 8.5

A. WARM-UP: *WITH YOUR CLASS*

Look at the ad in Figure 8.5. What product is being sold? What does the ad promise that the product will do for the consumer? Do you think that the advertiser is being honest? Why or why not?

B. DISCUSSION: *WITH YOUR CLASS*

Discuss what the phrase "truth in advertising" means. Try to answer the following questions during your discussion.

1. Do you think that most advertisers are truthful about their products?
2. What kinds of tricks do advertisers play on consumers so that they will buy?
3. Are there laws in your country to protect consumers?
4. What products have you bought that weren't what you expected them to be?

C. FOCUS VOCABULARY: *ON YOUR OWN*

On the lines below, write down any new words that you learn in class. Add to your list as you study about truth in advertising. Focus on new adjectives and nouns.

_____   _____   _____

_____   _____   _____

_____   _____   _____

_____   _____   _____

_____   _____   _____

D. READING: *Truth in Advertising*

Most people are suspicious of advertising. There are good reasons for this suspicion. After all, the purpose of advertising is to sell a product. Because of this, advertisements rarely point out the negative features of a product. Instead, they focus on the positive and try to make the consumer feel that he or she needs to buy the product. In order to do this, advertisers try to create an image of the product that will please the consumer.

Often the gap between that image and reality is very wide. In the past, advertisers created a positive image by making claims about what the product would do. Sometimes the claims about a product would be exaggerated, but often the ads were completely dishonest. Diet products promised that a person could eat any amount of food and still lose weight. Some people sold simple vitamins as cures for cancer or other diseases.

Today, laws keeps advertisers from making false claims about what their products can do. If they say that their product is better or stronger, they must prove it. Because of this, the image that is presented is more subtle. At one time, cigarette manufactures advertised that cigarette smoking was good for your health. Now, it is not possible for them to make this claim verbally or in writing, so instead, their ads show young, happy, and healthy people smoking their cigarettes. The form of the message has changed to obey the current laws but the message is the same—it is healthful to smoke.

To protect consumers from dishonest advertising, the government of the United States has passed several laws about false advertising. It is illegal to make untrue claims in advertising. The Federal Communications Commission, the United States Postal Service, and the Federal Trade Commission are government agencies that work to stop dishonest advertising.

E. COMPREHENSION: *On Your Own*

E.1. True or False

Read each statement about the reading and then circle *True* or *False*. If the statement is false, correct it.

1. Advertisers often give both positive and negative information about their products.	**True**	**False**	
2. There are laws to protect consumers from dishonest advertising.	**True**	**False**	
3. People can eat any amount of food and still lose weight.	**True**	**False**	
4. Ads in the past claimed that cigarettes were good for your health.	**True**	**False**	
5. Advertisers must prove their claims.	**True**	**False**	
6. Vitamins have been sold as a cure for cancer.	**True**	**False**	
7. There are several agencies that protect consumers.	**True**	**False**	

E.2. Completing a Chart: *On Your Own*

Use information from the reading above to complete the following chart. Discuss your answers with your classmates.

CHART 8.3

People are suspicious of advertising.

Reasons: 1._____

2._____

Ads in the past sometimes made false claims.

Examples: 1._____

2._____

Today, laws keep ads from being dishonest, but advertisers still present a positive image.

Examples: 1._____

2._____

There are government agencies that work to stop false advertising.

Examples: 1._____

2._____

3._____

F.   ORAL PRACTICE: *WITH YOUR CLASS*

According to the laws, advertisers cannot make false claims about their products. However, modern advertising is full of images and messages that give consumers misleading ideas. For example, a lotion that promises that it will "keep your hands younger looking" doesn't really promise anything. Think about it. What does the ad mean? Younger than what? What about an ad that says "three out of four doctors" prefer a certain type of cold medicine? Maybe this is true, but how many doctors did the advertiser ask? What do you think? Answer these questions.

1. Can you think of other examples of misleading advertising?
2. What kinds of images do you see on TV ads? Are they misleading?
3. Do you think this type of advertising is dishonest?
4. Should there be laws against ads that are misleading?

G.   ANSWERING SHORT ESSAY QUESTIONS: *ON YOUR OWN*

Look at the chart in Figure 8.6. Discuss the chart with your classmates. Next, read and think about each of the following questions below. Write three to five sentences to answer each question. Use the information from the chart and the readings in this chapter to complete your answers. Also, use your own knowledge.

1. What is a consumer survey? Give an example.

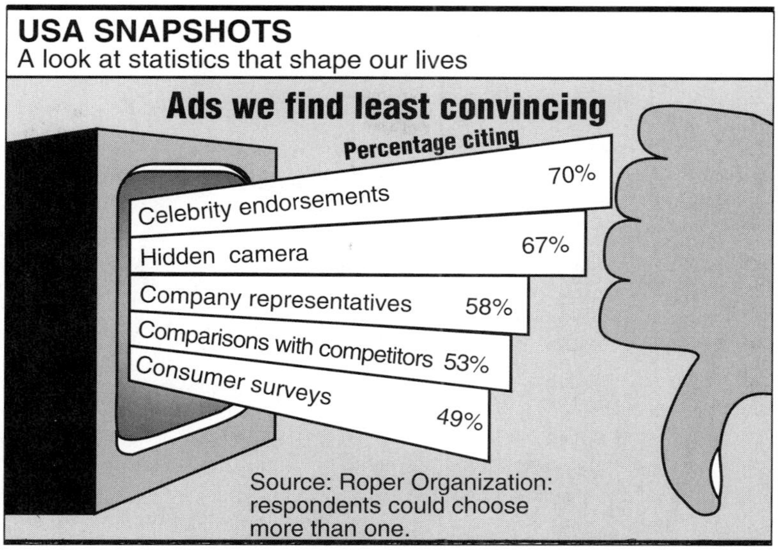

_____

_____

_____

_____

_____

_____

_____

_____

USA SNAPSHOTS
A look at statistics that shape our lives

Ads we find least convincing
Percentage citing

Celebrity endorsements	70%
Hidden camera	67%
Company representatives	58%
Comparisons with competitors	53%
Consumer surveys	49%

Source: Roper Organization:
respondents could choose
more than one.

REPRINTED BY PERMISSION OF USA TODAY

FIGURE 8.6

2. Do you believe ads that show famous people talking about the product? Why or why not?

_____

_____

_____

_____

_____

_____

_____

_____

3. What is the most honest type of advertising? Why do you think that it is the most honest?

_____

_____

_____

_____

_____

_____

_____

_____

_____

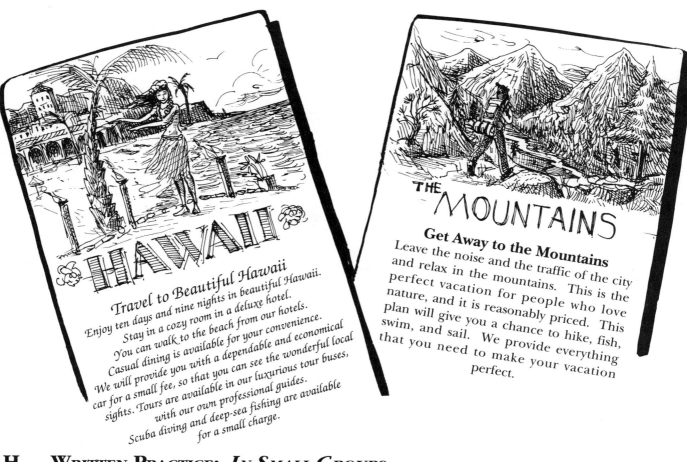

H. WRITTEN PRACTICE: *IN SMALL GROUPS*

Mr. and Mrs. Davis want to go on a vacation for ten days. They have looked at the ads and made lists of the costs for two different vacations. The first possibility is a trip to Hawaii. The second possible vacation is a camping trip in the mountains. Read the ad for each vacation.

Mr. and Mrs. Davis can't decide which vacation to take. They haven't had a vacation for a long time and they really want to relax and enjoy themselves. Go over the lists below carefully with your group. Write two statements about what Mr. and Mrs. Davis will or won't do if they choose one trip or the other for each item given. Share your answers with the whole class. Follow the model below.

VACATION #1 TO HAWAII		VACATION #2 CAMPING IN THE MOUNTAINS	
AIRFARE:	$850	AIRFARE:	NONE
HOTEL:	75 PER PERSON	HOTEL:	$15 CAMP FEE PER NIGHT
FOOD:	40 PER DAY PER PERSON	FOOD:	125 PER WEEK
CAR RENTAL:	50 PER WEEK	CAR RENTAL:	NONE
GASOLINE:	30 PER WEEK	GASOLINE:	75
TOURS:	50 PER PERSON	TOURS:	NONE
SCUBA DIVING:	125 PER PERSON	SCUBA DIVING:	NOT AVAILABLE

CLOTHING: FORMAL AND CASUAL

CLOTHING: CASUAL

ACTIVITIES: DINING, DANCING, SWIMMING, SCUBA DIVING, FISHING SHOPPING, SIGHT-SEEING, SAILING

ACTIVITIES: HIKING, FISHING, ROCK CLIMBING, SWIMMING, SAILING